REBELLION

A TELEVISION HISTORY OF 1798

REBELLION

A TELEVISION HISTORY OF 1798

Thomas Bartlett • Kevin Dawson • Dáire Keogh

GILL & MACMILLAN

Gill & Macmillan Ltd

Goldenbridge

Dublin 8

with associated companies throughout the world

© Thomas Bartlett, Kevin Dawson and Dáire Keogh 1998

0 7171 2761 3

Index compiled by Helen Litton

Design and print origination by O'K Graphic Design, Dublin

Colour reproduction by Typeform Repro, Dublin

Printed by ColourBooks Ltd, Dublin

This book is typeset in 11/18pt Bauer Bodoni

A catalogue record for this book is available from the British Library.

1 3 5 4 2

CONTENTS

1

IRELAND IN THE 1700s

The eighteenth century in Ireland was born from the embers of the Williamite Wars and from the paradox at the heart of the Protestant victory. For while the Catholic Jacobites had been defeated, the Protestant community was left with a real sense of its own insecurity.

At the root of Protestant fears lay the generous terms of the Articles of Limerick, which concluded the war but left the defeated Catholics in a far stronger position than might have been expected. As a contemporary poem ran, 'The conquerors lose, the conquered gainers are.'

The implications were clear. In Ireland, Catholic strength implied Protestant weakness: there could be no accommodation between the two. The Protestant state that was eighteenth-century Ireland owed its very life to the destruction of Catholic power. Yet the security of the state was threatened by Britain's continuing war with Catholic France and by the efforts of the Continental allies of the Catholic Pretender, James II (including the Papacy), to return the Stuarts to the throne.

It was from this pervasive background of fear that the notorious Penal Laws emerged—not from a desire to destroy Catholicism as a religion but rather as an attempt to reduce the political and military potential of Catholics. For this reason the political system, the legal profession and land inheritance were closed to Catholics. Though 70 per cent of the population, they were excluded from participation in the public and political life of post-Williamite Ireland and excluded also as a consequence from much wealth and most influence.

Yet the traditional view is a simplistic one. While the possession of power rested with the Protestants, there were many loopholes in the laws, which were exploited by Catholics. There were cases where Protestants held land for their Catholic relations, and there are many examples of Catholics making nominal conversions to Protestantism in order to hold land or to enter the professions. It is clear too that the Penal Laws were never fully implemented, apart from moments of international tension or domestic threat to the security of the Protestant state, as in 1715, 1720 and 1745 and during the War of the Austrian Succession (1740–48) and the Seven Years' War between Britain and France (1756–63).

A state ball at Dublin Castle

Catholic popular devotions, like this pattern at Glendalough, survived the effects of the Penal Laws.

That the Penal Laws were not always rigorously enforced is only one important point. Another is that they were applied not only against Catholics. When faced with the threat of a common Catholic enemy in the sixteen-eighties, Protestants of all shades had joined ranks. But once victory had been secured, in 1690 and 1691, the intense rivalries between the Protestant church and Presbyterian kirk re-emerged. As a result, in the north-east and in Belfast, where they were the majority, the Irish Presbyterians also suffered legal disabilities throughout the eighteenth century as Protestant Ireland attempted to buttress its position. While never excluded from Parliament or from the franchise, Presbyterians were barred from civil and military office, including municipal government, by the imposition of a sacramental test in 1704. As the century wore on,

Linen was the backbone of the Presbyterian north. This print from 1792 shows the beetling, scutching and hackling of the flax.

this was partially circumvented by annual Indemnity Acts. But there were continuing difficulties in the area of marriage and inheritance.

In these ways, Irish society was in effect divided into first, second and third-class citizens, with Protestants (Church of Ireland) forming the first division, followed by Presbyterians and finally by Catholics. More significantly, these divisions created tensions between the ruling class and the other groups. And in the long term these divisions in Protestantism were to be of great significance, since it could not be guaranteed for all time that Presbyterians would remain hostile towards Catholics.

So the paradox of the Williamite victory in 1690 remained at the centre of the Irish state nearly a century later. Protestantism was almost completely dominant; yet Protestants were desperately insecure. The fact that, for all their power, Protestants made up just 13 per cent of the population was fundamental to this condition. But so too was the nature of Protestant Ireland's relationship with Britain, the 'sister kingdom'.

After all, behind everything was the knowledge that the victory over the Catholic Jacobites in 1690 had not been theirs alone. The resolve of the Apprentice Boys of Derry in 1688 and defiant cries of 'No surrender' were all well and good, but the Williamite plight had been precarious until British ships famously broke the boom and lifted the siege.

The lessons of the episode were all too clear: the security of Protestant Ireland ultimately depended on the British connection. This fact became uncomfortably clear in the second half of the eighteenth century in the institutions at the centre of the Anglo-Irish relationship. While Ireland was constitutionally an independent kingdom, governed by the King, Lords and Commons of Ireland, in reality power rested in London. While the Irish Parliament could boast of its antiquity and rights, it was in fact humiliatingly subservient to Westminster. Its powers were limited by the terms of Poynings' Law

(1494) and the Declaratory Act (1720), which confirmed the British Parliament's claim to legislate for Ireland.

Ireland, in short, could not make its own laws. It could not even trade overseas without London's supervision. In this way Ireland, proudly a Protestant kingdom in name, was less independent than most of Britain's North American colonies.

Florence Court, Co. Armagh, one of the great Ascendancy houses

Rising tensions: the Parliament and the Castle

The question of political power in Ireland was, in a sense, a tale of two buildings, at either end of Dame Street: Dublin Castle to the west and the Parliament, a few hundred yards to the east in College Green.

The Irish Parliament was almost exclusively Anglican, since Catholics—70 per cent of the population—were excluded by law and Presbyterians—a further 13 per cent—were excluded by their social and economic status. The Parliament was representative, at most, only of the leadership elite of 17 per cent of the Irish population. In addition to this, it was in many ways under London's control. The (exclusively Anglican) bishops of

Dublin Castle

the Irish House of Lords were appointed from London, while the independence of the lay lords was affected by the fact that the government could create new peers in order to ensure majorities.

The House of Commons, the more important of the two assemblies, was made up of three hundred members. No fewer than 234 of these represented boroughs that were normally under the control of patrons who could be coaxed to support the government. There were two members for Trinity College, elected by the twenty-two fellows and seventy scholars, and sixty-four members who represented the thirty-two counties. These were the prestigious seats and the ones that were in effect the barometer of political opinion, because they were the most hotly contested. That said, the electorate in the county constituencies was restricted, not only by the Penal Laws but by the fact that the franchise was based on a property qualification. This meant that before 1793 the number of voters in each county was less than four thousand, except for County Down, which had an electorate of six thousand.

London, therefore, had the means to manipulate the Irish Parliament in its own interest. Nevertheless, a further layer of political management existed to ensure that the policies of the British government would be carried out. That task fell to the King's representative in Dublin, the Lord Lieutenant or Viceroy, an official whose period of tenure reflected the political fortunes of the parties in London. Usually a prominent English nobleman, he—and not the Parliament—in effect ruled Ireland. From the ancient seat of Dublin Castle, the Viceroy headed the Irish executive and was responsible for making senior

Henry Grattan

appointments in church and state. He was answerable to the Cabinet in London, not to the Irish Parliament in College Green—a fact that created deep resentment among the leaders of an Irish Protestant people that wanted the trust, responsibility and autonomous power that a loyal, Protestant and ancient kingdom felt it deserved. That emerging resentment, focused on the Parliament and giving rise to increasing demands for reform, was in truth the backbone of an Irish Protestant nationalism that became a powerful factor in the shaping of the turbulent politics of the seventeen-eighties and nineties.

Keeping closely to London's interests and direct instructions, Viceroys were usually able to manage the Irish Parliament through a shrewd use of patronage and pensions. Such manipulation, however, could create resentment and resulted in distinctions between what was regarded as an 'Irish interest', as opposed to the 'English interest' of the Viceroy. For almost a century the opposition to England's claim to legislate for Ireland had found expression in a small but vocal 'patriot' tradition, which had among its ideological champions William Molyneaux (1656–1698) and Jonathan Swift (1667–1745), who had memorably compared 'government without the consent of the governed' to slavery.

As the century progressed, this 'patriot' voice became the principal source of opposition to the policies of the administration. Ultimately, its leader in Dublin was the great parliamentarian Henry Grattan. The patriots were never very numerous: they were not a political party in the modern sense, nor had they a coherent policy. On occasion they were able to present a serious threat to the government, as in the early seventeen-fifties, when their opposition to a money bill created a crisis that prompted the administration to adopt a more 'hands-on' approach in Parliament. This development, however, provided a focus for resentment as Dublin Castle became more and more a symbol of the erosion of the constitutional rights of the Irish Parliament.

The Parliament House, drawn by its architect, Sir Edward Lovett Pearce, in the 1730s. Note the old front of Trinity College, which was replaced by the present building in the 1750s.

Rising tensions: the land and the secret societies

By the second half of the eighteenth century there was also great economic change, bringing new opportunities and prosperity but also conflict and tension.

The period after 1741 was marked by increasing prosperity. The traveller Arthur Young noted that since that time Ireland had 'made as great advances as could possibly be expected, perhaps greater than any other country in Europe.' The economy was based on agriculture, and while farming practices lagged behind those in England, the century witnessed a significant growth in the provisioning trade, brewing, and sugar production. There were regional differences: dairying was important around Dublin and in Munster, while in Ulster the linen industry had greatly expanded.

By this time, however, strains had begun to show. Ireland's population, estimated at 2½ million in 1725, had, after periodic famines, increased dramatically, doubling in the course of the century until it was about half that of Britain. But the effects of the agricultural growth had failed to filter down. Indeed, the combination of a rising population, the spread of land enclosure and the transfer of land to pasture created

Malton's view of Irish peasants gathering turf dates from 1790.

land hunger, bringing rent increases, sub-division, and frequently subsistence living.

The resultant rural tensions found expression in the growth of agrarian protest movements. Among the earlier groups were the Whiteboys (so called because they wore linen smocks), who arose in protest at the enclosure of common land in County Tipperary in 1761. They began by tearing down or 'levelling' fences, digging up pasture, and maiming animals. As the movement spread, their programme broadened to include opposition to excessive rents and to the tithes payable to the Church of Ireland. Similarly, their methods became more sophisticated, and groups were known to operate in groups of up to five hundred, some of them armed and many on horseback.

The Whiteboys were perceived by the establishment as representing a serious threat, particularly as their activities coincided with the Seven Years' War (1756–63), during which there were constant fears of a French invasion. It was a connection between Irish unrest and potential French opportunism that London and Dublin Castle never ceased to fear.

The Whiteboys established a pattern of rural protest. In Ulster their example was followed by the Hearts of Oak and the Steelboys; but of far more concern to the establishment was the Rightboy movement, which began in Cork in 1785 and gradually fanned out across Munster and south Leinster. The Rightboys opposed high rents, tithes, and other taxes, but in a novel departure they also made attempts to regulate Catholic dues and the fees charged by priests for baptisms, marriages, and funeral Masses.

Churches were 'visited', and unrepentant clergy had their chapels destroyed. Such activities were a source of acute concern for the Catholic hierarchy. Not alone was the church under attack from its own members but the violence jeopardised the political rehabilitation of Catholics.

Eager to pursue Catholic relief by moderation, the hierarchy excommunicated the Rightboys, just as they had censured the Whiteboys almost twenty years earlier. In a pastoral letter, Bishop John Troy of Ossory condemned them

> to everlasting Hell … When they shall be judged, may they be condemned … May their posterity be cut off in one generation. Let their children be carried about as vagabonds and beg and let them be cast out of their dwellings. May the usurers search all their substance and let strangers plunder their labours. May there be none to help them, nor none to pity their fatherless offspring. May their names be blotted out … Let their memory perish from the earth.

These tensions reflected bitter class and other divisions among the Catholic community, which, far from being united in suffering, was deeply divided on social and political issues. Such realities, however, failed to calm Protestant anxieties; indeed the violence was interpreted as further evidence of a Catholic plot. The British Home Secretary, Lord Sydney, expressed a belief that 'the Papists mean a separation of the two kingdoms and a popish king,' while in Munster sectarian memories of the past were resurrected in an attempt to preserve Protestant unity.

The fullest expression of these fears was given in a pamphlet written by the Anglican Bishop of Cloyne, Richard Woodward, entitled *The Present State of the Church of Ireland* (1786), which ran to four editions within two weeks of its publication. The bishop, pointing to the various threats to the establishment, stridently defended the connection between the Church of Ireland and the state. In an early sign of the common interest that was to be pursued in the seventeen-nineties, such sentiments aroused the opposition of Catholics and Dissenters, both resentful of their exclusion from the political process.

On the face of it there was little to connect the agrarian outrages of the Whiteboys and Rightboys with the sullen resentment by the Protestant leadership of their impotent Parliament and its subordination to London and the Castle. But the connection was there; in their own way these two distinct and opposite groupings—nations within a nation in post-Williamite Ireland—were unhappy with the late eighteenth-century status quo. So too in their prosperous but disenfranchised circumstances were the articulate, organised Presbyterians of Belfast and the north-east. In each of the three strata of Irish society, as the eighteenth century lengthened there was a growing desire for change. So far they were separate constituencies; but what would happen if they came together? And what catalyst might occur that could bring such an event about?

The American crisis: a first Atlantic revolution

As the century reached its three-quarter stage the isolated developments in Ireland suddenly acquired a context: the revolt of Britain's colonies in North America.

The reasons for the American revolt may lie ultimately in a slowly gathering sense of American identity and self-interest among the inhabitants of the thirteen colonies along the Atlantic seaboard. But the fighting itself was provoked by Britain's insistence on the

The British surrender at Yorktown, Virginia, in 1781

right to make laws and raise taxes, and on the colonies' refusal to comply. When Britain enforced its will in arms, George Washington led the colonial army in resistance. Had French aid and professional Prussian training not assisted Washington's ill-formed army in the early days, the British might quickly have won. But the Americans resisted and pushed back and after six years forced a final and humiliating surrender by the British at Yorktown.

The British officer who formally submitted to Washington at Yorktown was Charles Cornwallis, later Lord Cornwallis; in 1798 he would be Viceroy of Ireland. Also in the British force that day was a young officer named Francis Needham, who would later gain a mixed reputation at the Battle of Vinegar Hill near Enniscorthy, County Wexford.

Not at Yorktown but also in the British army during that campaign was a young officer of the highest rank in the Anglo-Irish nobility: Lord Edward Fitzgerald, son of the Duke of Leinster. He would be a United Irish leader in the spring of 1798. It was a convulsive moment in history for men and nations; and, as Cornwallis led the British laying down of arms, his military band somewhat presciently beat out the tune of 'The World Turned Upside Down'. The impact of the American events echoed round the world, and in Ireland they reverberated loud and long.

The initial consequences for Ireland were economic. As the revolution turned into war, London imposed an embargo on Irish trade in an effort to guarantee supplies for its forces. Added to these restrictions, financial pressures of war created an economic depression in Britain, the shock waves of which plunged Ireland into recession. These were, in any context, conditions conducive to political agitation.

Yet the economic effects were only the beginning; the fortunes of Britain's American colonists had important implications for all sections of Irish society. Observers in Ireland followed developments with great interest, and Irish opinion clearly divided on the imperial crisis. It was inevitable that events in America should arouse interest in Ireland, not least because of the numbers of Irish people that had settled in the colonies—particularly, and significantly, among Ulster's Presbyterians.

Ties were particularly strong between Ulster and the North American colonies. Perhaps as many as forty thousand emigrated from the province to America between 1769 and 1774. Such emigration justified the claim of the radical Presbyterian minister and subsequent United Irish leader William Steele Dickson that there was 'scarcely a

Protestant of the middle class amongst us, who does not reckon kindred with the inhabitants of that extensive continent.' It was these familial ties and the important trade links between Belfast and New York and Philadelphia that fostered sympathies among the Presbyterians of Antrim and Down—themselves victims of political disabilities—for the oppressed colonists.

There were also important constitutional issues. The grievances of the colonists were bound to strike a sympathetic chord with the Irish patriots. Both parties appeared to share a common cause, which the American intellectual and politician Benjamin Franklin had identified on his visit to Ireland in 1771. Entertained by both 'courtiers and patriots,' Franklin recalled his impressions of the latter:

> I found them disposed to be friends of America, in which I endeavoured to confirm them, with the expectation that our growing weight might in time be thrown into their scale, and by joining our interests with others, a more equitable treatment from this nation [England] might be obtained for them as well as for us.

Many of the later United Irishmen shared this enthusiasm for the American revolt. William Drennan, a Belfast Presbyterian who was then a medical student at Edinburgh, later one of the founders of the United Irishmen, viewed America as 'the promised land', while William James MacNeven, who was to become the most senior Catholic United Irishman, in adulthood recalled how as a young boy he had seen Americans in handcuffs and how from that moment on he had followed the war with passion.

William Drennan

Given the shared sympathies of the Irish patriots and American colonists, the American war quickly had the effect of bringing to the surface many unsettled and unsettling elements in the Irish political climate—a climate in which parliamentary reform and better representation were already on the agenda.

The effective management of the Irish Parliament was crucial, and successive Viceroys attempted to secure the support of the Parliament for British measures in America. This

The American Declaration of Independence

was a difficult task, since many in the Parliament shared Franklin's view that the cause of America was the cause of Ireland. During debates in late 1775 members argued that British suppression of America would set a dangerous precedent for Ireland. As George Ogle argued, if you vote the Americans to be rebels, for resisting taxation where they are not represented, what can you say when the English will tax you?

For the moment, however, Ogle was in the minority. The Americans were described as 'rebels' in a loyal address to the king, and the Parliament voted to allow the withdrawal of troops to serve in the disturbed colonies.

The reaction of Irish Catholics to the American revolt was more complex. While they did not have the same kinship links with America, there was a significant representation of Irish Catholics in Washington's army, and there is some evidence in Irish-language poetry of support for the colonists. For the most part, however, whatever their sentiments, Catholics believed that their interests would be best served by stressing their loyalty to the Crown. The previous ten years had, after all, brought a great improvement in the political fortunes of Catholics as the political debris of the Williamite struggle finally began to clear. To begin with, the defeat by Britain of Catholic France in the Seven Years' War (1756–63) reduced the threat of invasion from the French-based remnants of the Catholic Jacobite interest. Meanwhile the death of the Jacobite heir and Old Pretender, James III, in 1766 allowed for greatly improved relations between Britain and the Holy See. This in effect marked the end of the Jacobite cause, but it also reduced British suspicion of Catholic reliability and cleared the way for Irish Catholics to pledge their loyalty to the now Papally approved British Crown.

This process of rehabilitation received a further boost in 1774 with the passing of the Quebec Act, which guaranteed civil rights to the Catholics of Britain's newly acquired Canadian colony. This established an important precedent, and the American war provided Ireland's Catholics with an opportunity to stress their loyalty. Streams of loyal addresses poured into Dublin Castle; frequently these were relayed to London, while in August 1779 the Viceroy, the Earl of Buckinghamshire, published one in the London Gazette 'in order that the courts of Paris and Madrid and all Europe might know how firmly [the Catholics] were attached to His Majesty's person and government.' More immediately, the war provided a vital opportunity to express their allegiance. What better way to demonstrate loyalty to the Crown, after all, than by joining the military?

Thus it was that Irish Catholics began to enlist in the British army, and individual Catholics, including Lord Kenmare, offered bounties to encourage them to join the ranks.

Technically, of course, it was illegal for Catholics to be armed, and there was little explicit reference to such recruits in government publications.

Still, Catholic loyalty did not go unrewarded. As early as April 1778 the British Prime Minister, Lord North, had promised 'justice to Ireland' for its loyalty during the war, and within five years Ireland's Catholics benefited from two important relief measures. Both of these were initiated by the London government and carried through the Irish Parliament in College Green in the face of stern opposition from Protestant diehards. Under the terms of the Relief Acts of 1778 and 1782 the principal restrictions on land ownership and on the practice of religion were removed. The acts had a very definite purpose: they were not a panacea for the problems of all Ireland's Catholics, rather they were intended to encourage their leaders, the priests and gentry, to beat the recruiting drum. Catholic relief may have been a reward for Catholic loyalty; but it was also intended to yield military rewards for London.

The American crisis: the rise of the Volunteers

And thus it was in the military arena that the political effects of the American Revolution began to coalesce and in turn transform the Irish political scene.

Military priorities were paramount, because the American war had placed great demands on Britain's resources. In Ireland the problem was particularly acute, since the war had necessitated the withdrawal of four thousand Irish troops to serve as 'armed negotiators' in North America. Their departure left Ireland dangerously exposed, not only to foreign invasion but also, in an age when the military fulfilled police functions, to the violence of the Whiteboys or like-minded groups, such as the Oakboys and Steelboys. Traditionally, in times of emergency, such as the threat of invasion during war, a militia force was called out. This was a civilian army whose task it was to police the country and to perform garrison duties. Their officers held commissions from the Crown, and they were paid for their services. In 1778 the need for the Militia was obvious. Britain was at war, troops had been withdrawn, and French, Spanish and American ships threatened Ireland's coastline.

Yet as the American crisis deepened, the government was pouring its money into the war and had little left for home security. Strapped for cash, it resisted calling out the

An infantry Volunteer, c. 1778

Militia. In these critical circumstances the vacuum was effectively filled by a private army—one that was to become the crucible of revolutionary politics in Ireland.

It began in March 1778, when the people of Belfast formed their own Volunteer company, in line with tradition. Before long their example was followed throughout Ireland. Their commander, Lord Charlemont, recorded a stylised account of their formation:

Abandoned by Government in the hour of danger the inhabitants of Belfast were left to their own defence and boldly and instantly undertook it; associations were formed, arms were purchased; uniforms were provided; officers were chosen; parades were appointed and every diligence exerted towards the necessary acquirement of military skill and discipline.

So far, this was a traditional response. But what became significant about the Volunteers was not the circumstances of their formation but the political independence and influence they quickly exerted. Unlike the Militia, the Volunteers were a private army, loyal to the Crown but not under its control. They resented the way in which the government had exposed Ireland to danger and were determined to refuse it any share of the credit for the country's salvation. This raised serious questions about the legality of this private army, but in the moment of crisis the government had no choice but to go along with it.

The Volunteers presented an impressive spectacle as they drilled in their colourful uniforms. At their height

Lieutenant Hyndman in Volunteer uniform

The Dublin Volunteers in College Green, 1779

they boasted 100,000 members. Of these one-third were from Ulster, where kinship with the American rebels was strongest. In the country the leaders were drawn from the gentry, while in the towns, corps were formed by occupational groups: Dublin, for example, had a lawyers' corps and a goldsmiths' corps.

In many ways the Volunteers were exclusive—Henry Grattan described them as 'the armed property of the nation'—but in other respects they were surprisingly open. Presbyterians quickly rallied to their banners, for, much as they sympathised with the Americans, they hated the French. Significant too—and in line with the new atmosphere for Catholics—was the decision of many companies to admit Catholics to their ranks. But there were other novel aspects to Volunteering, notably its democratic character and the unprecedented practice of electing officers and of reaching decisions by consensus. The uniforms were traditional; the attitude and ideas were new.

The political potential of the 100,000 Volunteers was immediately apparent to the patriot leadership, which sought to exploit this powerful independent body; many MPs, including Grattan and Flood, appeared in Volunteer uniform. In this way Volunteering provided a focus for patriotism, always an important element in Irish politics but hitherto without a regular organisation through which it could make its presence felt.

But Volunteering now not only provided a focus but also represented in its armed ranks stark evidence of Protestant strength and determination. In November 1779 the Dublin Volunteers gathered before the statue of King William III in College Green to demand 'Free Trade or a Speedy Revolution'. It was a demonstration made possible by the conditions of the American war and politically imaginable only because of the influence of the Americans themselves.

Lord North's government in London conceded these initial demands. But, hungry now for reform and impressed by their own armed, persuasive force, the Volunteers became more ambitious. As early as December 1780 the Newry Volunteer Company began to question the value of the concessions. What use was a relaxation of trade restrictions when they could be reimposed by the British at will? What Ireland needed was the sole right to make its own trade laws, and indeed all its own laws.

Grattan addressing the Irish House of Commons

The Volunteers now pressed ahead in an attempt to liberate the Irish Parliament altogether from the long-standing and troublesome restrictions of Poynings' Law. This campaign reached a peak in February 1782, when a delegate convention of 304 Ulster corps met in Dungannon—significantly, in the Presbyterian hall—and ratified what was in effect a political manifesto asserting the sole right of the King, Lords and Commons of Ireland to make laws for Ireland.

The Dungannon resolutions provided the Volunteers with a definite programme. However, by themselves they did not achieve immediate results. In the Dublin Parliament the patriots, under Grattan, unsuccessfully proposed legislative independence. Yet in less than a month circumstances were greatly altered by the collapse of Lord North's government at Westminster. The Whigs took office, under the Marquis of Rockingham. In opposition they had supported the patriots, so they could hardly oppose Grattan's demands for a restoration of the rights of the Irish Parliament.

In Dublin Castle the new Viceroy, the Duke of Portland, rapidly became aware of the desire for change. In April 1782 he informed London of the existence of an overwhelming consensus (which the United Irishmen would later attempt to re-create):

> the merchant, the tradesman, the manufacturer, the farmer, the labourer, the Catholic, the Dissenter, the Protestant: all sects, all descriptions of men … unanimously and most audibly call upon Great Britain for a full and unequivocal satisfaction.

The demands were answered with the passing of a body of legislation in London that repealed the Declaratory Act (1720) and amended Poynings' Law.

There was a wave of euphoria. Ireland's constitutional claims had been settled, and Grattan, the hero of the hour, received a unanimous vote of £50,000 from the Irish House of Commons. It was the peak of an extraordinary phenomenon, born of slowly kindled political frustrations, lit by the spark of the American war.

In one sense it was a modest revolution. It aimed to redefine and restore the legislative power of the kingdom of Ireland and to limit, not end, British influence. It was Protestant and Presbyterian and avowedly loyal and therefore had little to do with the needs of the Catholic majority. And, as was to become evident, even the gains apparently made under Grattan proved short-lived.

But in other ways it was momentous. The Volunteer phenomenon showed how the first revolution in the Atlantic world had quickly coloured the Irish situation. The Volunteer ranks had brought Protestant and Presbyterian together in joint disaffection, with united purpose. Catholics had been admitted on the fringes. And, given a forum in which political opinions could be mobilised and voiced, the Volunteers had rapidly become more radical.

Finally, there were the College Green demonstrations: political demands placed before the Parliament by a massed, uniformed body carrying banners and wielding guns. Speedy resolution, or speedy revolution. It was militant radicalism, united politics. And, in the view of some, it was also the moment when the gun entered Irish political affairs. The moment passed, but the lesson was not forgotten.

Chapelizod, Co. Dublin: eighteenth-century order . . .

. . . and disorder: a painting entitled Elegant Figures Drinking and Smoking in a Brothel

The rise of the Catholic question

Soon the hollowness of the so-called 'Constitution of 1782' was all too apparent. Cool analysis revealed that the powers Britain had signed away remained within Britain's unilateral power to reimpose.

The influential faction led by Henry Flood first identified a flaw in the legislation. They rejected the simple repeal of the Declaratory Act, demanding instead an unequivocal renunciation of Britain's claim to legislate for Ireland. This came in April 1783, but other thorny issues remained unresolved, concerning external affairs and trading rights. Of more immediate concern to radical opinion, however, was the question of reforming the Parliament itself, particularly the necessity of making constituencies more representative and making the Castle administration answerable to the Parliament.

These remained potent issues into the middle of the seventeen-eighties. The remnant of the Volunteers were in the vanguard, but their continued failure to achieve 'a more equal representation of the people in parliament' reflected the divisions within Irish political society.

The Volunteer movement in effect stalled, and its energies dissipated as the erstwhile reformers bickered over how to proceed.

From a British perspective, the extension of the rights of the Irish Parliament made political management both more important and more difficult. These new circumstances challenged the abilities of successive Viceroys. They also emphasised the need to strengthen the executive arm of the government by the appointment to key offices of talented and reliable Protestants—members of Parliament like John Foster, John Fitzgibbon, and John Beresford, who served as an informal 'Irish Cabinet'. This talented but deeply conservative troika became a vital element in the government of Ireland and shared London's opposition to parliamentary reform.

That was one road-block in the way of further or fundamental reform. But there was another, and in a sense it was very much the reformers' own dilemma. The most

A rural kitchen interior

formidable barrier to political renewal remained, as Drennan put it, 'the rock of religion and indulgence to Catholics.' At the core of the whole Volunteer phenomenon was the reformers' call for a new Irish constitution based on representation. But the more advanced radicals now demanded to know how a constitution could represent the nation if three-quarters of the nation—the Catholics—were still excluded.

It was a fundamental dilemma. Some of the Protestant leaders, such as Grattan, realised the necessity of embracing the Catholic community. 'The question', he argued, 'is whether we shall be a Protestant settlement or an Irish nation … So long as the penal code remains we can never be a great nation.'

Many other Protestants, however, remained to be convinced that Catholics were reliable. History had long taught them otherwise, and there was a general acceptance of the identification of Catholicism and despotism. For many Protestants, Catholics were simply incapable of living in liberty: they were unfit for power. As the outspoken reformer Sir Edward Newenham MP put it, 'We are for freedom, they are for despotism.'

But it was not simply an issue of theology or political principles. It was also about land and power. There was a belief that the concession of the vote to Catholics would be followed by demands for a return of their confiscated estates. It was a thought to give pause to any wavering liberal. The reformers contributed to their own downfall in the middle of the seventeen-eighties by placing the

John Foster, one of the Dublin Castle 'troika'

Catholic question on the political agenda. The advanced reformers, by pressing for Catholic inclusion, had driven deep divides through their ranks. As long as those divisions remained, the conservative Irish establishment, personified by Beresford, Fitzgibbon, and Foster, was secure.

And yet within the kingdom of Ireland tensions existed and were growing. These tensions were reflected all too clearly in County Armagh, where Anglicans, Dissenters and Catholics were present in almost equal numbers. The county became the cockpit of strife, where the broader political tensions of the country found vent in what appeared on the surface as sectarian violence. The reality was more complex, because the struggles between the political ascendancy and the dispossessed were played out in a rural setting. Central to the struggle was a new, shadowy and predominantly Catholic secret society founded in 1784 known as the Defenders. There had been secret societies before (and would be again), but this one was to become widespread and radical and would have a pervasive influence on events up to and including 1798.

While the Defenders' secretive and violent methods resembled those of the Rightboys and earlier protest movements, they had a definite political agenda. Their aim was not only to remove immediate grievances, such as excessive rents and tithes, but to bring down the Ascendancy and to reverse the effects of the plantations of the seventeenth century by overthrowing the land settlement, the social hierarchy, and the established church. As a contemporary account put it,

> they can never forget that they have been the proprietors of this country ... They look upon or talk of the English settlers as not of their nation [and wish] to plant the true religion that was lost since the Reformation.

A view of Carrick-on-Suir, Co. Tipperary. Agrarian tensions ran high in Tipperary in the second half of the eighteenth century.

Defenderism, with its political agenda, quickly spread in a secret network across south Ulster, into north Leinster and towards the midlands. Its activities unnerved Protestants everywhere. Moreover, the upper levels of the Ascendancy were now to be shaken by a crisis on the throne itself.

The madness of King George

In November 1788 King George III became seriously mentally ill. The king's insanity sparked a constitutional crisis, since it raised the question of the nomination of a regent to rule in his absence.

Within the Irish Parliament the crisis enveloped the conservative establishment, which faced an immediate challenge from the patriot opposition. For months in Westminster a fierce debate over the royal crisis had raged between the Prime Minister, William Pitt, and the Whig opposition. Now the Whigs' patriot allies in Ireland saw in the crisis an opportunity to express the independence of the Parliament in College Green.

Claiming to itself the right to nominate a regent, the Irish Parliament drew up an address calling on the Prince of Wales to assume his father's duties. This decision was a bold assault on accepted procedure. The Viceroy refused to transmit the address to England, and the Parliament appointed commissioners to do it instead. Only the king's sudden recovery saved London from an embarrassing challenge to its authority in Ireland.

Yet while the status quo had been preserved, the episode gave a new impetus to radical politics. Not only did the crisis expose the hollowness of the so-called 'triumph of 1782' and the unequal nature of the Anglo-Irish relationship but it led to the establishment of a formal Whig party, which aimed to reduce the corrupting influence of Dublin Castle. Beyond College Green, Whig clubs were established in Dublin and Belfast and several other towns, not only to marshal support for candidates in the elections of 1790 but to revive the brave spirit of Volunteering. These developments, though they awaited one further injection of revolutionary energy, were to lead directly to the watershed establishment of the United Irishmen.

The core of reformist thought was already clear. The draft manifesto of the Belfast club, drawn up by Dr Alexander Haliday, was a classic statement of Whig ideology, the teachings of John Locke and the principles behind the 'Glorious Revolution' of 1688. Government, it argued, was based on a contract between 'the governors and the governed, instituted for the good of the whole community.' 'Majesty' rested 'in the people,' and the King was merely the 'servant of the people.' The document upheld the values of civil and religious liberty, but while it stressed the 'sacred and inviolable connection with Great Britain,' it laid specific emphasis on the rights and independence of the Irish Parliament.

> The subjects of this realm are of right free, and independent of, the authority of any parliament or legislative whatsoever, save only the parliament of Ireland, that is to say, the king of Ireland, and the lords and commons of this realm.

The lobby of Waterford courthouse, 1784

It was a radical reform manifesto, albeit a loyal one. On the surface, however, little came of the Whig clubs, which Tone later dubbed 'oyster clubs'. The clubs enjoyed election victories in Dublin but did not threaten the government majority. However, the real significance of the clubs lay in the impetus they gave to politics, the focus they provided for reformers, and the way in which they prefigured the United Irishmen. But the final dynamising element, greater even in its impact than the American war that had so affected Ireland, was now about to occur.

France, 1789: a second Atlantic revolution

If the constitution of 1782 had been won on the back of the American war, events unfolding in France now opened up a host of new possibilities. News from France quickly dominated the Irish press. Within weeks of the opening of the Estates-General in May 1789 the term 'French Revolution' began to appear in the newspapers. With the same startled fascination that was general throughout Europe, the Irish attempted to absorb the enormity of events that represented the greatest political convulsion since the Reformation.

The collapse of the French monarchical government, Europe's most powerful, happened with remarkable speed. Louis XVI, bankrupt and in need of new tax revenues, failed to secure fiscal compromises from the privileged classes. When the Estates-General was called to resolve the crisis the middle classes themselves revolted. Within weeks a generation of radicals had emerged to resist heavy-handed royal suppression and whip up popular fury. The toppling of the Bastille was simply the visible prelude to a new order, conspicuously based on the principles of rational, representative government and the Rights of Man.

At first in Ireland there was little consensus on how this news was to be interpreted. But as time progressed and attitudes hardened, the Revolution became the 'test of every man's political creed.' Commentators were divided between 'democrats' and 'aristocrats'. The cause of the aristocrats was championed in Edmund Burke's *Reflections on the Revolution in France*, while the reformers looked to Tom Paine's response, *Rights of Man*—reprinted in at least four Irish newspapers—which described the age as 'an age of revolutions in which everything may be looked for.' For the radicals, such sentiments had an obvious appeal, reflected in the decision of the 'Whigs of the Capital' to publish a cheap edition of twenty thousand copies.

The Declaration of the Rights of Man

The storming of the Bastille in Paris, 14 July 1789

The chemistry of the French events began to work on the Irish political mix. Concepts of 'liberty, equality and fraternity' were obviously attractive to radical Anglicans and Catholics; but among the Presbyterians of Antrim and Down they had a more vivid and immediate resonance. There were obvious comparisons between their plight and that of the Third Estate in France. Ulster Presbyterians had long been educated in Scotland, where they had been formed in the spirit of the Enlightenment. Presbyterianism too of its very nature was a dynamic creed, democratic and anti-hierarchical.

These factors made Dissenters receptive to the 'French principles', but more immediately their participation in ten years of Volunteer and subsequent Whig agitation had served as a political apprenticeship. Belfast's Presbyterians sought redress of their grievances and an end to their treatment as second-class citizens and to the monopoly of the city's politics by the Protestant Marquis of Donegall. The Presbyterians as a cohesive, self-aware Irish community had been significantly politicised and were becoming ever more active. Given the concentration of Presbyterians in the north-east, it was no exaggeration to say that Ulster in the last quarter of the eighteenth century was becoming the political engine in the drive towards reform.

In July 1790 the Volunteers marched again, and in Belfast—not to celebrate the Battle of the Boyne but the fall of the Bastille. Perhaps most significantly, news from France was beginning to diminish the anti-Catholic bias that during the seventeen-eighties had divided the reformers. While traditional prejudice had insisted that Catholics were unfit for liberty, in France they had now overthrown the most despotic regime in Europe. Not alone had they brought about a revolution but French Catholics were enjoying greater liberty than that offered by Britain's vaunted constitution.

The Presbyterian minister George Whitefield preaching at Lurgan, Co. Armagh, 12 July 1751

31

The stage was now set for a new departure in Irish politics. Yet before this could be achieved it was essential for the radicals to convince as many as possible of the reliability of the Catholics. This task was taken on by a young Dublin barrister, Theobald Wolfe Tone, who in August 1791 wrote the most influential pamphlet in Irish history. It was entitled *An Argument on Behalf of the Catholics of Ireland*, and it aimed to allay Protestant, but particularly Presbyterian, fears.

Tone's argument was blunt. He made no attempt to shield his scorn for the 'Revolution of 1782', which he described as a 'most bungling imperfect business.' The whole episode had failed, he believed, because it had 'left three fourths of our countrymen slaves as it had found them.' More than that, the Volunteers and the reform movement of the eighties had been fruitless because 'they were built on too narrow a foundation.' The way forward, Tone argued, was to embrace the Catholic cause.

He urged those who remained in fear of Popery to look to France, where the Pope had been burned in effigy. 'Where is the dread now of absolute power? ... where is the intolerance now of popish bigotry?' More than this, not alone were Catholics capable of liberty but there could be no liberty in Ireland unless the religious sects joined together in opposition to the 'boobies and blockheads' who governed them. The choice facing Protestants, Tone believed, was simple:

> on the one hand, reform and the Catholics, justice and liberty; on the other, an unconditional submission to the present and every future Administration ... who may indulge with ease and safety their propensity to speculation and spoil and insult.

What Tone was proposing was a radical alliance, unthinkable just fifteen years earlier, before the American war: Catholic, Protestant and Presbyterian united in making a new Ireland. Moreover, given the effect of France on Irish political thought, Tone's forceful pamphlet itself seemed likely to make the alliance finally happen.

For the British government the implications of Tone's radical vision were nothing less than horrific. The Foreign Secretary, Lord Grenville, wrote to the Viceroy, Westmoreland:

> I may be a false prophet, but there is no evil that I should not prophesy if that union

takes place and at the present moment and on the principles on which it is endeavoured to bring it about.

In Tone's optimistic argument and the Foreign Secretary's conservative response are apparent the polarised positions that would finally come to arms in 1798. But in the heady days of 1791, moves were already afoot to forge Tone's novel union. Bastille Day in 1791 was marked by auspicious celebrations in Belfast. The radicals of the city were to the fore, and they were joined by others from further afield, including Tone.

BELFAST VOLUNTEERS.

BY command of the committees of our refpective corps, jointly convened by fummons, we requeft the attendance of all their members in full uniform, at the White Linen-Hall, to-morrow, precifely at 12 o'clock, for the purpofe of expreffing their joy at the fuccefs of the arms of the French Republic, by firing three feu-de-joies.

THE volunteers requeft the attendance of their fellow-citizens, at the Donegall-Arms, at feven o'clock faid evening, to join with them in declaring their fentiments on this aufpicious event.

Monday, 29th October, 1792.

HU. M'ILWAIN, Sec. Belfaft Troop.
JOHN RABB, Sec. Firft Belfaft Vol. Com.
JAMES M'CLEAN, Sec. Belfaft Vol. Com.

A notice to Belfast Volunteers to assemble for a celebration of French victories in the Revolutionary War

In the months that followed, the Presbyterian William Drennan, a long-time radical, developed a plan for a new political society. He had tired of the moderation of the Whigs, whom he dismissed as an 'aristocratical society', an accurate assessment, since they aimed not at a truly representative parliament but rather at one that reinforced the monopoly of the Anglican elite. The Whigs, he believed, had little interest in the people; 'when the people come forward, these men draw back.' What was needed, Drennan argued in his famous letter to his brother-in-law Samuel McTier, was 'a benevolent conspiracy—a plot for the people. The Brotherhood its name—the Rights of men and the Greatest Happiness of the Greatest Number its end—its general end Real Independence to Ireland, and Republicanism its particular purpose.'

Over the summer Drennan co-operated with Samuel Neilson and the Belfast Volunteers, who advanced the plan. In October 1791 Tone was invited to Belfast for the inauguration of this new club. At its inauguration there were just twelve members, ten of them Presbyterians, including Drennan, Neilson, and the brothers William and Robert Simms. Tone was not technically a founder-member but joined officially within days, along with his close friend Thomas Russell, a former army officer (and later magistrate). Henry Joy McCracken, a young firebrand from a draper family, also soon became involved.

Theobald Wolfe Tone

It was Tone, the charismatic and clubbable Trinity College graduate and frustrated barrister, who from the beginning made a particular mark. It was he who not only gave the club its name, the United Irishmen, but also drew up its resolutions and declarations calling for 'an equal representation of all the people in parliament.'

The radical reformers who grouped together in Belfast under the United Irish banner were, by Irish standards, unlikely revolutionaries. Though not landed gentry, by any reckoning they were among the educated and privileged of Protestant and Presbyterian Ireland.

In the following month the veteran Dublin radical and Volunteer politician James Napper Tandy established a United Irish Society in the capital, which in its two-and-a-half years of existence as a legal society attracted a membership of four hundred. Its proceedings were dominated by lawyers and by those connected to the university, but the membership was mixed: there were a few country gentry, but it was mainly composed of professionals and city merchants and textile manufactures. At first the membership of the Dublin society was predominantly Protestant, but among the founding members were two of the leading Catholic activists, Richard McCormick and William MacNeven. Other early and leading members included Archibald Hamilton Rowan, a wealthy ex-Volunteer and reformer of some standing who had spent time in America and France, and Thomas Addis Emmet, a brilliant lawyer, the elder brother of Robert Emmet.

The Society of United Irishmen called for

—the promotion of constitutional knowledge, the abolition of bigotry in religion and politics and an equal distribution of the Rights of Man throughout all sects and denominations of Irishmen;

—a brotherhood of affection, an identity of interests, a communion of rights and an union of power among Irishmen of all religious persuasions;

—immediate, ample and substantial justice to the Catholics and when that is attained, a combined exertion for a reform of parliament is the condition of our compact and a seal of our communion.

These aims reflected the long pedigree of Irish radicalism, which was rooted in Whig principles, the ideas of John Locke and the contract theory of government that had justified England's 'Glorious Revolution' of 1688. Accordingly, the United Irishmen claimed sovereignty for the people:

We can give no truer definition of slavery, than that state in which men are governed without their consent, and no better description of freedom than that not only those

A view of Kilmallock, Co. Limerick

who make the law, should be bound by the law, but those who are bound by the law should share in the making of it.

Such sentiments contained echoes of Swift and the patriot tradition, but equally they reflected the transformation that the American revolt, Volunteering and the French Revolution had brought to Irish radicalism. This combination gave the United Irish ideology—in its early stages at least—its curious character, which appealed to the traditions of the 'British Constitution' while condemning the corrupting influence of England: 'We have no national government; we are ruled by Englishmen, and the servants of Englishmen.'

James Napper Tandy

That said, the original United Irishmen stopped short of demanding complete separation, even though this was clearly Tone's intention from as early as July 1791.

The new society was avidly propagandist. Apart from its own deliberations, it sought to politicise public opinion in an unprecedented way. As Thomas Addis Emmet put it, they aimed 'to make every man a consummate politician.' This would be achieved in a threefold action that Drennan summed up as 'declaration', 'publication', and 'communication'.

Thomas Addis Emmet

Cheap editions of important texts, particularly Paine's *Rights of Man*, were produced, as were distilled compilations of Enlightenment thinkers such as Locke, Godwin, and Voltaire. This task was facilitated by the large numbers of printers and booksellers within the United Irish ranks, but novel channels were used to distribute political tracts, newspapers, and handbills, which were often packed in bales by shopkeepers.

Archibald Hamilton Rowan

Newspapers were a vital part of United Irish propaganda, particularly their own *Northern Star*, founded in Belfast in January 1792. It was the principal organ of the society, and it is estimated that each of the four thousand copies of each issue reached at least ten people through public reading. In his *Memoirs*, Miles Byrne, the United Irish leader, by then serving in the French army, recalled the joy he experienced as a young man listening to the news of French victories being read from the papers at the chapel of Monaseed in rural County Wexford.

In a similar way the United Irishmen employed ballads in their evangelical drive; there were at least four editions of their popular *Paddy's Resource*, containing songs that James Hope's fictitious Squire Firebrand believed 'infects a whole country and makes them half mad, because they rejoice and forget their cares, and forget their duty, and forget their betters.'

Catholic politics

Just as the reform movement and Volunteering were transformed by events in France, so too were Catholic politics fired by the new spirit. Since the 'Revolution' of 1782 the leadership of the Catholic Committee, composed largely of Catholic gentry and the episcopacy, had given way to a new, aggressive bourgeois generation, including founders of the Dublin United Irish Society such as Richard McCormick and John Keogh, who began to demand emancipation as a right, not a reward to be sought with deference. In July 1792 Tone was appointed assistant secretary to the Catholic Committee, thus establishing an important bridge to the United Irishmen.

The 'brotherhood of affection' was becoming a reality. As far as an anxious London was concerned, some measure of Catholic relief was necessary if this union was to be sundered. This ploy had worked during the American war, when the Relief Acts of 1778 and 1782 had helped prevent an emerging alliance between the Catholics and Volunteers. The problem now was that there was such anti-Catholic feeling within the Irish Parliament that London could not risk precipitating a crisis by beginning radical changes.

Political concessions were out of the question. In fact a petition in February 1792 by the Catholic Committee for admission to the franchise was rejected in the Irish House of Commons by 208 votes to 25. The most that London could offer Ireland's Catholics was

Entry of the Speaker into the Irish Parliament, 1782. Parliamentary feeling was strongly opposed to Catholic concessions.

minor concessions and their admission to the legal profession; but even that meagre sop created furore in the House of Commons. Although the measure was carried, through the skilful management of the Viceroy, insults were hurled at the members of the Catholic Committee by diehards, who dismissed them as 'shopkeepers and shoplifters' and 'men of very low and mean parentage.' Tone was particularly incensed at the depiction of the committee as a 'rabble of obscure porter-drinking mechanics.'

Such insults goaded the Catholic Committee to action. Determined to refute suggestions that Catholics 'disavowed and despised them,' the committee decided to hold a great representative assembly of the Catholics of Ireland, modelled on the Volunteer Conventions of the seventeen-eighties.

Throughout the summer Tone and Keogh criss-crossed Ireland, securing the election of delegates to this gathering, which met in the Tailors' Hall, Back Lane, Dublin, in December 1792. The assembly of 273 representatives sent a shock not only to the

Ascendancy but to the entire political system in Ireland, because in this so-called 'Back Lane Parliament' the Catholics presented themselves as the people of Ireland, demanding emancipation as their right. Even the usually conservative Archbishop Troy of Dublin in his address to the delegates declared his support for emancipation and the determination of the clergy to rise or fall with the people. And if any further statement of the Catholic Committee's resolve was needed, the gathering appointed delegates to present their appeal directly to the king, demanding nothing less than 'the total abolition of all distinctions' between the people of Ireland. This was a calculated decision, a blatant rejection of the Viceroy and the Dublin Castle administration, reinforced by the fact that the delegates travelled to London by way of Belfast, where the radicals of the city drew their carriage through the streets in triumph.

Catholic relief—and European war

Relations between the Irish radicals and the London and Dublin establishment were always likely to be difficult. But just as overseas events had transformed Irish politics in the previous fifteen years, they now conspired again to dash any hope of a reasoned debate on reform in the seventeen-nineties.

The Cry of Liberty and the Departure for the Frontier, 1792. The Revolutionary War galvanised the young French republic.

The French Revolution had taken many turns since the storming of the Bastille in July 1789. While there had been a general welcome in the capitals of Europe for the tumult in Paris, the increasingly radical nature of the revolt created a spirit of reaction. The implications of the French experiment were all too apparent for Europe's rulers, because of its universal quality: as the *Northern Star* put it, the Revolution concerned not merely the fate of France but that of the world.

The execution of King Louis XVI on 21 January 1793

The early stage of the Revolution brought the Declaration of the Rights of Man, containing principles enunciated by the Americans. But the French moved far beyond that moderate position, sweeping away the institutions of church and state through a series of measures, including the Civil Constitution of the Clergy (July 1790), which in effect abolished the Catholic Church, and constitutional reforms culminating in the declaration of a republic in September 1792. When Louis XVI was imprisoned, then guillotined, in early 1793, the new French state took on an alien and threatening demeanour to many outside.

European establishments were horrified by events in France. At the heart of the matter were the differences between irreconcilable systems of government, one based on dynastic considerations and the acceptance of inequality, the other founded on notions of popular sovereignty. Even though in May 1790 the French National Assembly had declared its intention of living at peace with the other countries of Europe, armed conflict was perhaps inevitable.

Once France declared war on Austria in April 1792, the continent drifted into battle. Soon Prussia too became involved, and most observers judged—correctly—that it was only a matter of time before Britain was drawn in to the struggle. With this possibility looming (it became a reality on 1 February 1793), the pacification of Ireland was an obvious priority for William Pitt; not alone would discontent disturb the war effort, but in war, Catholics would be badly needed to fill the ranks of the British army. And the rivalry of Britain and France over centuries, coupled with the new ideological differences and rapid advances in the technology of war, meant that the new war would be one in which Britain would be fighting for its very survival.

So for Britain the security issues were fundamental. The government believed, as Edmund Burke had argued, that substantial relief measures would undermine the United Irishmen and Irish radicalism, because, if satisfied, the Catholics would abandon the Presbyterians and fall in behind their natural leaders, the counter-revolutionary clergy and gentry.

For all these reasons, the fears of Dublin Castle and the opposition of the ultra-loyalists in the Irish Parliament were brushed aside: imperial concerns took priority. In April 1793 London pushed through a relief measure that granted the vote to Irish Catholics on the same terms as Protestants. The passing of the bill brought euphoria to Dublin; the city was illuminated, and one observer reported that 'Dublin is now as a noon day, every bell is chiming and every heart delighted.'

It was not long, however, before this joy receded, as Catholics considered what had been withheld by the bill. The concessions were far less than the Convention had demanded. As Tone argued, if the Catholics deserved what was conceded, they were equally entitled to what was withheld. Even the ultra-loyalist Speaker of the Irish Parliament, John Foster, acknowledged that it was 'vain to imagine that admission to the elective franchise does not draw with it the right of representation' in Parliament.

There would be no more progress in this direction, nor were those calling for parliamentary reform to be satisfied. British security was paramount: war was no time for constitutional experiment; nothing could jeopardise the war effort. The government embarked on an offensive against political radicals, and a raft of legislation was adopted in an attempt to secure the kingdom. These measures included laws to limit the importing of arms, prosecutions for seditious libel, and an unpopular act to raise a militia of fifteen thousand men. In addition a Convention Act was passed, which outlawed political assemblies, and the Volunteers were suppressed.

In one sweep the Castle had undermined the political reform movement. The Convention Act deprived the radicals of their most effective channel of political agitation, while the suppression of the Volunteers deprived them of their organisational network and means of rallying support. It was an end, the government intended, to fifteen years of armed pressure.

This strengthened armoury was essential, because in addition to the pressures of war the spread of Defenderism had brought violence to much of Ireland. The society was based on tightly knit cellular units, which were held together by oaths reflecting their anti-Protestant, millenarian aspirations. But more ominous for Dublin Castle was their support for the French:

> The French Defenders will uphold the cause
> The Irish Defenders will pull down the British laws.

So far the harsh counter-measures against the Defenders—speedy executions, mass arrests, and the shipment of suspects for service in the Royal Navy—had not proved effective. By the summer of 1795 Dublin Castle believed that as many as fifteen counties were contaminated by the Defenders. Their growth was most marked in areas of heightened political and sectarian tension, where the Ascendancy was most aggressive.

From 1795 onwards the government relied increasingly on terror. The most notorious example of this approach was the judicial execution of a Meath Defender, the schoolmaster Laurence O'Connor, sentenced to death in 1795 for Defender activities. He was put to death in grisly fashion in Naas, and the political meaning of the event was underlined by the presence of the Viceroy as a witness. O'Connor's body was disembowelled and quartered and his head placed over the jail, on Viceregal instructions, as an example to others.

At a non-official level the loyalist response was equally determined. This was particularly evident in County Armagh, where in the summer of 1795 there was renewed violence between the Defenders and their Protestant equivalent, the Peep o' Day Boys. Out of one clash, the 'Battle of the Diamond' near Loughgall, emerged the Orange Order. Formed to defend perceived loyalist interests against the depredations of the Defenders, the order quickly spread throughout the countryside as a counter-revolutionary force. Violence spread likewise.

The government had not promoted such sectarian tensions—it had criticised them; but from 1796 onwards it moved to exploit the Orange Order, confident that such tensions

Christ Church Cathedral, Dublin, in the late eighteenth century

could stem the 'uniting business'. As Thomas Knox, the military commander in mid-Ulster, put it in a despatch to Dublin Castle in August 1796,

> we must to a certain degree uphold them, for with all their licentiousness, on them we must rely for the preservation of our lives and properties should critical times occur.

For this reason the authorities turned a blind eye to the terror inflicted in Ulster and the expulsion of thousands of Catholic families to Connacht and elsewhere. As Edmund Burke observed, 'Catholic Defenderism was the only restraint upon Protestant Ascendancy.'

The Orange Order spread rapidly in mid-Ulster especially, where it acted as a buffer, checking the growing alliance between the United Irishmen and the Defenders. This nexus was a vital part of the radical plan, since Defenderism provided a broad base for what might without them have been simply a bourgeois movement. The United Irishmen, however, were not slow to exploit sectarian fears among the Catholic population; the Orange bogey became an important part of their propaganda, and there are many instances of fabricated Orange oaths to massacre Catholics.

The political polarisation, added to the spread of violence, was a far cry from the optimism of the United Irish manifestos of 1791 and 1792. There was, however, a moment of opportunity during 1795 with the arrival of Earl Fitzwilliam as Viceroy. His appointment raised hopes for parliamentary reform. He had many Irish connections, and he was a disciple of Edmund Burke and known to share his mentor's pro-Catholic sentiments. The new Viceroy recognised that many of Ireland's problems stemmed from the influence of Dublin Castle. If Ireland was to be saved from revolution, the system would have to be reformed. But more than that, Catholics would need to be emancipated if they were to become reliable citizens.

Earl Fitzwilliam

In a sense what he proposed was constructive counter-revolutionary policies. In his enthusiasm, however, he moved too fast. Within days of his arrival he dismissed the ultra-conservative members of the Castle administration, the faction dubbed the 'junta' by the reformers. Their dismissal, and rumours of immediate emancipation, encouraged by Henry Grattan, aroused opposition in London. Fitzwilliam was recalled.

Radical Ireland was stunned. Fitzwilliam was escorted to the quay by crowds dressed in black, while the people took the horses from his carriage and pulled it to the waterside. Little wonder that commentators believed that Ireland was then on the brink of civil war.

Camden, who succeeded Fitzwilliam as Viceroy

Suppression and French aid

If Fitzwilliam's departure created sorrow, the arrival of his successor brought riot and death to the streets. The new Viceroy, Earl Camden, arrived with very clear instructions. There was to be no more constitutional experimentation; in fact his instructions were specifically to 'rally the friends of the Protestant interest.'

The shutters came down. Grattan's emancipation bill was easily defeated, and in a cynical but successful move the state sponsored a Catholic seminary at Maynooth. It was a clear attempt not only to remove the anti-Catholic tag from the government but to buy off the bishops and ensure their support for the regime. The Maynooth grant, however, was resented by the Catholic laity, who saw it as no more than a sop for the lost emancipation bill; in this way it served to further distance Catholics from their conservative hierarchy. The seventeen-nineties display one of the great ironies of Irish history, that two such institutions as Maynooth and the Orange Order were products of the same counter-revolutionary policy.

Under Camden, straight counter-revolution became policy. The government had already formed a national network of Militia forces loyal to the Crown. Now munitions and numbers were increased. Peacetime laws, including *habeas corpus*, were suspended.

Magistrates and soldiers were given a freer hand under the terms of an Insurrection Act: it provided the death penalty for administering an unlawful oath and allowed whole counties to be 'proclaimed' or placed under military control.

The United Irishmen undertook, with success, to infiltrate the Militia. Faced with such disaffection and the ever-present threat of a French invasion, the Castle sponsored a part-time Yeomanry, to be raised, drilled and commanded by reliable Ascendancy leaders. The force was not exclusively Protestant—in fact the young Daniel O'Connell was a member—but from the beginning it had a definite Protestant character. In 1798 its role would be crucial.

The changing temper of the age had brought a dramatic transformation in the United Irishmen; by 1795 it bore little resemblance to the society established four years earlier. Certainly parliamentary reform was still its primary goal—in fact its most comprehensive political agenda was published as late as 1794. Nevertheless divisions had emerged in the

McArt's Fort on the Cave Hill above Belfast, where Tone and other leading United Irishmen made their separatist vow in 1795

ranks over how far to go. For its part, Dublin Castle as early as December 1792 had believed that the United society would accept France's offer to liberate unfree peoples.

There were those, like Drennan, who took a moderate line, arguing that the society should remain political, acting as a pressure group. There was also a more radical element, which included Tone, Neilson, and Russell, who believed that real change could only come about through radical action. They were particularly active in Ulster, where, as we have seen, links had been established with the Defenders, and Militia units had been infiltrated.

It was the arrest in April 1794 of Rev. William Jackson, an agent of the French government, that marked the moment of decision. Among his papers was found a memorandum prepared by Tone concerning French military aid. Negotiations had begun, and the Castle and the British now realised it.

Tone's future was uncertain. In the chilly, security-dominated atmosphere of the time he could have been in mortal danger. But his charm, his network of friendships in official Dublin and perhaps plain luck allowed him to escape lightly. He made a statement to the Castle about his part in the Jackson affair, in return for which he would not be tried but was to quit the kingdom. On 20 May 1795, accompanied by his wife, Matilda, and their children, Tone and his brother Arthur left Dublin for Belfast, whence they were to sail for Philadelphia.

Unwittingly, the Castle's deal with Tone had facilitated his appointment as United Irish emissary to France. In meetings with Russell and Thomas Addis Emmet it was agreed that Tone's stay in the United States would be brief. In his diary he recalled that his task was to 'set off instantly for Paris and to apply in the name of my country for the assistance of France to enable us to assert our independence.' In Belfast he met the leading radicals of the city, who were convinced of the need for military action. Before his departure, Tone, Russell, McCracken and a select group made a vow at McArt's Fort on the Cave Hill. They promised 'never to desist in our efforts until we subverted the authority of England over our country and asserted our independence.' It was a pivotal moment, symbolising the shift in atmosphere from the heady idealism of 1791 and signposting the road ahead to the carnage and desperation of 1798.

A few days later, on 13 June 1795, the Tone party set sail on the *Cincinnatus* for America.

Tone and the French

Arriving at Philadelphia in August, Tone met Archibald Hamilton Rowan, who had come from France. The United States was neutral in the European war, but American politicians were divided between a pro-British Federalist Party and the pro-French Democratic Republicans.

The French minister in the city was Pierre Adet, and Tone made it his business to meet him at the earliest opportunity. On 10 August the Irishman presented his credentials, which reflected not only his own pedigree but that of Irish radicalism: these consisted of certificates not only from the United Irishmen and the Catholic Committee but also from the Belfast Volunteers. At first the minister was sceptical, but he asked Tone (the arch-propagandist) to prepare a memorandum. Tone's detailed production reflected his discussions with Belfast's radicals. It stressed the strategic importance of Ireland and the sympathy of the Irish for the French cause. But, more importantly, it emphasised the extent to which Britain relied on Ireland, which supplied the bulk of its provisions, two-thirds of its navy, and 180,000 soldiers. Ireland, Tone argued, held the key to the destruction of England and to the 'Liberty of Mankind.'

Lazare Carnot, 'the organiser of victory'

To achieve this, Tone requested arms, ammunition, artillery, money, and a force of not less that twenty thousand men. These troops, however, would not form an invading army: rather they would act as Ireland's allies. Immediately on landing, the French would issue a proclamation to that effect, announcing their arrival and the end of the 'ancient tyranny of [Ireland's] oppressors.' This proclamation would also call on the Irish people to elect provisional deputies, who would form a government, guaranteed by the French Republic, subject to only one condition: that it would be 'totally separated and independent of England.'

Adet agreed to forward the memorial to Paris. Two months later he did so, with a positive covering letter. Little came of Tone's efforts; frustrated, exiled from Ireland and unable to travel to France, he considered settling in Princeton, but a combination of circumstances changed his mind.

There was his obvious dislike of the Americans, whom he described as 'selfish, churlish ... totally absorbed in making money ... half English, half Dutch with the worst qualities of both countries.' Of more significance, however, was the news he received in November 1795 in a letter written by John Keogh two months previously informing him that Ireland was ripe for a French invasion. Armed with this intelligence, he

Hoche's proclamation announcing the Irish expedition

returned to Adet, who now supported a mission to France. Accordingly Tone, alias James Smith, set sail from New York on 1 January 1796.

Since the heady days of 1791 France had offered help to other nations wishing to assert their liberty. Paris was a focus for foreign radicals, and the Foreign Ministry in the Rue du Bac and the Ministry of War in the Rue de Varennes were besieged by various delegates pleading their case. But a succession of bad experiences in Belgium, Poland and Holland had made the French sceptical of foreign radicals, especially those like the 32-year old Tone, making grand promises on behalf of uncertain allies. Nevertheless, the timing of his arrival was fortunate. The stability of the Directory depended largely on the successes of the French armies. The war was now at a critical juncture; an armistice was in operation with Austria, but France's implacable enemy, Britain, remained in arms.

Tone's proposals offered substantial possibilities. The French had offered support to Ireland as early as 1792–93, and Nicholas Madgett, an Irishman in the Foreign Ministry, assured him that Ireland still figured in France's thinking. At this point, however, the Directory's plans for Ireland were not to Tone's liking, since they were intent not on

The port of Brest

liberating Ireland but on fomenting a civil war there that would drain England's resources, much as the counter-revolutionary rising in the Vendée had sapped France's.

Yet in spite of all the obstacles, and his own lean credentials, Tone succeeded eminently in his military diplomacy. It was an extraordinary achievement. Tone correctly identified the importance of Lazare Carnot, the Director with responsibility for war, who at that time was at the height of his career. Amazingly, Tone convinced Carnot to abandon his original plans for Ireland. His promises were verified through French contacts, particularly Edward Fitzgerald, Arthur O'Connor, William Duckett, and other United Irishmen in Hamburg, and by 19 June 1796 the

General Lazare Hoche

Directory approved plans for an invasion of Ireland, substantially on Tone's terms. The aim of this mission was outlined by Carnot: it was to

> detach Ireland from England, to reduce England to a second-rate power, and to take from it much of its maritime superiority. There is little point in elaborating on the advantages to France that Irish independence would bring ... the fall of the most irreconcilable and most dangerous of our enemies. I see in it tranquillity for France for centuries to come.

Tone's other great contact was Lazare Hoche, the 28-year old general whose only rival in reputation and glory was the young Napoléon Bonaparte. The command of the invasion of Ireland was entrusted to Hoche, and he and Tone became firm friends. Dressed in his new French military uniform, with the rank of adjutant-general, Tone travelled to Brittany with Hoche in the winter of 1796 to complete his extraordinary mission: to bring a French invasion force to Ireland.

Bantry

It was not until 16 December that a fleet sailed from Brest, consisting of seventeen ships of the line, thirteen frigates, and twenty transports. Between them they carried 14,450 troops and over 40,000 stand of arms. There was also a military band, with instructions to teach the Irish the revolutionary songs of the 'Marseillaise' and 'Ça Ira'.

Hoche's great fear was the Royal Navy, acknowledged as the finest on the seas. Although Britain had little intelligence of French plans, it was constantly on guard against French expeditions. Outside Brest was a British naval group vigilant for French activity and determined to effect a blockade; but a fierce easterly wind pushed the French fleet rapidly out of port, past and out of sight of the waiting British. It was a remarkable break-out for so large a body of ships.

It was, however, the last piece of good fortune the expedition was to enjoy. For the wind that had aided the French at the first now became their worst enemy. Fierce storms blew up, breaking up the French fleet. Worst of all, Hoche himself, aboard the command vessel, was blown out into the Atlantic and out of contact with his ships. Signals by flare or cannon could not be attempted, for fear of alerting the British navy.

The destruction of the French fleet by storm in Bantry Bay

As the remaining ships came close to Ireland, the instructions were opened and the landing-place identified. It was to be Bantry Bay.

Dublin Castle had no warning. The first word came from a landlord named Richard White, who looked out from his terrace over the waters of Bantry Bay on 22 December and saw warships forcing their way towards the shore against stormy winds. He sent word urgently to the authorities that up to sixty French ships were making towards land. No Crown force of any size stood nearby to repel the feared French army.

This advantage was of little avail to the intending invaders. The fleet was in disarray. Hoche was by now utterly lost and would not be seen again during the expedition. One-third of the ships were still out in the Atlantic; the rest were braving the storms in the bay. On board the eighty-gun flagship *Indomptable* the uniformed Tone could only watch as Hoche's deputy, Grouchy, attempted to carry out the invasion plan.

But the Revolution had purged the navy of many of its best and bravest sailors. For eleven days incessant winds, poor seamanship and indecision prevented a landing. Thousands of soldiers and tons of weapons and powder lay just offshore. On land there was no sign of the British; but neither were there the thousands of Irish revolutionaries that Paris had been told lay in wait to greet the French and to join them.

Beaten by fierce storms and without Hoche to lead them, the French stood offshore from Christmas Eve to New Year's Eve. Seasick and increasingly low on supplies, the men's initial high spirits plummeted and they became near-mutinous. Tone repeatedly feared drowning. Yet he wrote in his diary that he felt he could have touched the shore with his hands. 'We were near enough to toss a biscuit ashore,' he wrote as the realisation of failure dawned, adding: 'England has not had such an escape since the Spanish Armada.'

After ten days the French despaired and fled Bantry. On their way home they lost seven ships in addition to the three lost on the outward journey, and perhaps a thousand more men. Britain had had its narrowest escape from invasion for two hundred years. Richard White, the Ascendancy landlord who gave the warning of the French fleet, was made Earl of Bantry; but for Tone there was only despair.

2

BANTRY AND ITS AFTERMATH

98

The security dilemma for Dublin Castle

Throughout the seventeen-nineties, the central security dilemma for Dublin Castle had been that no single policy could deal with the twin threats that confronted it: the prospect

Blackrock Castle, Co. Cork: the bays and inlets along the south coast were seen as likely landing places for the French.

of an invasion of Ireland by revolutionary France, and the growing threat of insurrection from within Ireland. The near-miss of the French invasion effort at Bantry threw the dilemma into sharp relief. But it did not solve it.

On the one hand, it was well understood by the generals that the defence of Ireland required a concentration of soldiers—along with adequate supplies of tents, biscuits, and cattle—at or near the likely invasion sites, so that an enemy on landing could be immediately attacked and, they hoped, repulsed by a well-equipped force. In addition, conventional military and naval thinking decreed that a descent on Ireland—if it came at all—would most probably take place on the south coast or the north-east. (The east coast, with Dublin as its prize, was ruled out on the grounds that no French fleet would run the huge risk of being trapped in the Irish Sea and then destroyed by the Royal Navy. Similarly, the west and north-west coasts, between Galway Bay and Lough Swilly, were in general discounted, because of tricky seas, distance from France, and huge supply problems if an army did manage to struggle ashore.)

On the other hand, by 1795 Dublin Castle faced a serious threat of insurgency. The Defenders, the Catholic secret society, had their origins in County Armagh in the seventeen-eighties, but during the nineties they had spread far beyond that county. By 1795 Lord Camden, the newly appointed Lord Lieutenant, could list thirteen counties, in south Ulster, north Leinster and north Connacht, in which Defenderism had gained a hold.

What lay behind Defenderism was something of a mystery: alongside agrarian grievances over tithes, taxes and rents were found anti-Protestant slogans, millenarian aspirations of a world turned upside-down, and—ominously for Dublin Castle—explicit expressions of support for the French.

Dublin Castle would have preferred to concentrate its forces against further French invasion. But so far harsh counter-measures against the Defenders had not proved effective. Throughout 1795 and 1796 arms raids, killings and robberies had continued unabated. In addition, and ominously, by 1796 persistent reports were reaching Dublin Castle that the Defenders were making common cause with the United Irishmen.

The Castle's security dilemma lay in the fact that counter-insurgency tactics to deal with the threat of the Defenders called for a dispersal of the forces under its command, with the consequent deployment of hundreds of tiny garrisons throughout the disturbed areas. But such a dispersal meant inevitably that if an enemy such as the French should land in force, it would be many days before a large force could be assembled to repel them.

In the years before Bantry Bay, Dublin Castle had concluded that the main threat to the security of Ireland came not from a French invasion but from the rural insurgency of the Defenders. The theoretical possibility of a French attack on Ireland was dismissed when set beside the actual record of attacks, assassinations, arms seizures and sectarian brawling throughout large areas of Ireland. The likelihood of a French invasion was therefore pooh-poohed, and a policy of counter-insurgency was given precedence over one of defence. As a result, even though there were frequent rumours that the French were planning some sort of raid on Ireland—and indeed there was plenty of evidence that the United Irishmen were seeking their assistance—there had

Edward Cooke, Under-Secretary for Ireland

been little or no preparation to resist them should they effect a landing.

It is clear that by this time a healthy confidence with regard to French naval capabilities had yielded to a dangerous complacency; and this shift almost brought disaster to the British empire. After Bantry, a shocked Dublin Castle and military establishment were forced to review their thinking.

The forces of the Crown in Ireland

What were the forces at the disposal of Dublin Castle in late 1796? In the face of mounting evidence of an alliance between the Defenders and the United Irishmen, Dublin Castle had responded uncompromisingly. New laws were put through the Irish Parliament providing for the imposition of curfews, the arrest of suspects, and harsh penalties—including death—for tendering or taking oaths. *Habeas corpus* remained suspended, and provision was made for proclaiming certain districts under military control.

Then there was espionage. An extensive spy network was, with difficulty, set up, and by late 1796 the Under-Secretary, Edward Cooke, found himself at the centre of a spider's web of informants, informers, agents, and spies. The administration's problem had never been a lack of intelligence, for there had always been a constant flow of reports into Dublin Castle; its difficulty had lain rather in the absence of proper evaluation of the incoming intelligence, and in this respect Cooke's capacity for cool appraisal and dispassionate assessment was vital to the counter-insurgency policies embarked upon in the late seventeen-nineties.

This family group, painted in 1750, symbolises the confidence of the Ascendancy at mid-century. This was later shaken by agrarian protests and the rise of both the Defenders and the United Irishmen.

These new draconian laws, and the Castle's intelligence network, were backed by a huge increase in the range and number of the soldiers available to Dublin Castle. In 1793 an Irish Militia had been established. Based on the territorial division of the county, and consisting of Catholic rank and file and (mostly) Protestant officers, the Militia were seen both as a defence force and a sort of nursery for the regular army.

The decision to form the Militia had met an immediately hostile response. Within months there were violent protests in almost every county; in eight weeks as many as 230 people were killed in the violent protests and in the harsh measures adopted to suppress them. There were grave fears about the force's reliability, which the United Irish attempted to justify by infiltration and subversion; indeed Tone, in promoting the idea of an invasion of Ireland to the French authorities, had argued 'to a moral certainty' that the Militia would desert to a French force if it disembarked in Ireland.

A

SERMON

PREACHED AT

St. MARY's, KILKENNY,

SUNDAY THE 7th of JANUARY, 1797,

ON THE

PROVIDENTIAL DISPERSION

OF THE

ENEMY's FLEET,

AND THE

DELIVERANCE OF THIS KINGDOM

FROM

THREATENED INVASION.

BY THE

RIGHT REV. THOMAS LEWIS O'BEIRNE, D.D.

LORD BISHOP OF OSSORY.

Published at the Desire of the RECORDER, MAYOR and CORPORATION of the City of KILKENNY, and of the PORTRIEVE and BURGESSES of IRISHTOWN.

The cover of a sermon preached by the Church of Ireland Bishop of Ossory at St Mary's, Kilkenny, on 7 January 1797 in thanksgiving for the failure of the Bantry Bay expedition

By December 1796 the Militia had a strength of some eighteen thousand. Alongside these there were in late 1796 some nine thousand Fencibles. These mostly came from Scotland, and they had arrived in Ireland throughout 1796 to facilitate the departure for the West Indian theatre of the regular army regiments then stationed in Ireland. The Fencibles were unimpressive militarily, being frequently composed of those considered unsuitable for the regular army. The demands of the West Indian theatre had been remorseless, and as a result of the policy of substituting Fencibles for regulars there were only some 3,500 regular cavalry and about 1,600 regular infantry in Ireland in late 1796.

Finally there was the recently established Yeomanry force. Approval for the setting up of an Irish Yeomanry had been grudgingly given by Dublin Castle in September 1796, and there had been a rush to form both cavalry and infantry corps. The duties of the

Yeomanry were to police their own counties and, in the event of an invasion, to assist the Militia, Fencibles and regulars by keeping an eye on the (allegedly) disaffected within their areas. Such people, it was felt, might think of taking advantage of the alarm and stage diversionary attacks.

The original caption on this drawing reads: 'The gallant Irish Yeomen dispersing a gang of Irish incendiaries and murderers.' The Yeomanry were much feared in the countryside.

The Yeomanry, contrary to received opinion, was not an exclusively Protestant, much less Orange, force, but it was disproportionately recruited in Ulster, and in that province it rapidly acquired a reputation for militant loyalism; this notoriety soon infused the whole. By December 1796 there may have been some twenty thousand Yeomen, but they were new, untried, and not yet fully equipped.

These forces, in total some fifty-three thousand, were divided into five districts, approximating to northern, southern, eastern, western, and central. They were under the overall command of Lord Carhampton, infamous for his dragooning of Connacht in late 1795, during which large numbers of suspected Defenders had been summarily sent to serve in the Royal Navy.

The Irish administration had reasons for anxiety concerning its armed forces. Firstly, they were widely dispersed. There were important garrisons only at Blaris, near Belfast, and Loughlinstown, near Dublin. If the French could successfully disembark a sizable force it would take many days to mobilise an army capable of opposing it.

Secondly, widespread dispersal of the soldiers had been detrimental, it was generally agreed, to discipline. Frequently the men were billeted beyond the control of an officer, and often they were encouraged to go beyond what the law would permit in pursuit of rural insurgents. Moreover, as a result of slack discipline a number of the Militia regiments in particular had been infiltrated by both the United Irishmen and the Defenders.

Thirdly, there was much criticism both of the officers in the Irish regiments and of the more senior regular officers. Many of the Irish officers were absentees, who often owed their appointment to political influence, while regular officers were held to be generally uninspiring, barely adequate to prosecute counter-insurgency policies, and mostly too incompetent to serve elsewhere.

A view of Loughlinstown Camp, the chief army camp near Dublin

Reaction to the Bantry Bay expedition

The French expedition to Bantry Bay was a failure. Nonetheless the United Irishmen,

The young General Bonaparte at the Bridge of Arcole in November 1796. The rise of Bonaparte and the demise of Carnot and Hoche spelt the end of real French interest in further Irish adventures.

while disappointed, were not downcast, and, understandably, they entertained high hopes that the French would come again, perhaps with an even larger number of troops. The United Irishmen were particularly pleased that the famous 'General Hock', victor over 'the Vendians and despot priests,' had been in command, and they were reassured by the reported quality of the soldiers ('all picked desperate men') that he had with him. None now could doubt that there was a genuine alliance between the United Irishmen and the French. Some United Irish units began gingerly practising the operation of miniature guillotines (using captured cats). And perhaps now was the time, as some claimed, to start polishing up one's French?

Enthusiasm for the French Revolution remained strong in Presbyterian Ulster. This print shows a 1792 celebration of Bastille Day in Belfast.

The truth was that United Irish optimism was grossly misplaced. French commitment to an Irish invasion peaked at Bantry and then rapidly receded. For them, the expedition

63

had been a disaster. They had in all lost four ships and 1,500 men to the Atlantic storms and to enemy action, and their plans had been exposed to the British. Moreover, the great promises made to them by Tone seemed to have proved hollow. There had been no evidence in Bantry of a United Irish army waiting onshore, as Tone had promised. The French troops and sailors who survived the expedition had endured hunger, illness, and great danger; there was near-mutiny at talk of going to Ireland again.

Tone's support in the revolutionary government and in the armed forces began to diminish. Lazare Carnot, the person in the Directory most in favour of an Irish invasion, lost his place and his power. And what of Lazare Hoche, the charismatic general and rival to Bonaparte, who had been Tone's greatest support? Hoche was dying. Shipwrecked en route from Bantry, he had been forced to swim ashore near Brest through the cold and violent Atlantic waves. His health was broken; in a little over eight months, to Tone's great distress, he died. The rising Bonaparte would take far less interest in Ireland or its strategic value against Britain; with Hoche's and Carnot's removal went much of Ireland's hope for French assistance on the grand scale.

And yet in Ireland and in London the French near-miss proved a potent catalyst to political thinking and military preparations. Irish loyalists were horrified by the expedition: sermons were preached and prayers offered for Ireland's deliverance, and thanks given for the second 'Protestant wind' in a century to discomfit loyal Ireland's enemies.

Yet while Bantry had boosted United Irish morale and provided it with a propaganda coup, Dublin Castle too could draw some comfort from the outcome. The spirit evinced by the soldiers and Militiamen as they had set off against the French had been pleasing; and the newly formed Yeomanry earned plaudits for the way various corps took over garrisons in order to free regular troops for the expected campaign.

Moreover, the 'zeal and loyalty displayed by the inhabitants of the south' during the short-lived emergency was welcome. The Catholic Bishop of Cork, Dr Moylan, had promptly issued an address enjoining obedience and loyalty on his flock, and as the soldiers and Militiamen marched south in the dead of winter to attack the French it was reported that 'the peasants in the counties of Cork and Limerick anticipated their wants by preparing potatoes for them on the road' and by clearing snow in their way. 'In short,' concluded the Viceroy, Camden, 'the general disposition of the people through the south and west was so prevalent that I have no doubt had the enemy landed their hope of assistance would have been totally disappointed.'

These things apart, however, there was precious little to celebrate. Shocking evidence had been provided about French intentions and capability. They had come in strength; they could come again. Even the loyal response of the populace in Munster was held to be suspect. 'Had a complete landing been effected,' noted the Under-Secretary, Cooke, 'I fear that there would have been another tale'; while General Dalrymple in his report on the emergency scoffed: 'While our Eagles head to the enemy, the people will probably act with us: turn your standards and they will probably turn with them.'

Moreover, the military response to the crisis had been generally undistinguished and on occasion chaotic. The army staff was at sixes and sevens in mobilising its forces: Camden reckoned it would take 'a few days' to assemble a force of nine thousand near Cork and a few days more to increase that number to fourteen thousand. In the meantime Carhampton, the commander-in-chief, conceded that Cork and possibly Limerick might fall to the French. Certainly General Dalrymple, in command in Cork, admitted he had no plans to defend the city: 'a diversion is all to be expected' from his men. And Colonel Vallancey, commanding the Tyrone Militia in Limerick, had no high opinion of General Smith, who was charged with organising that city's defence: 'I cannot give you any account of the confusion that reigned there,' he wrote to a correspondent. Who could say what the consequences would have been if these cities had fallen and the French had begun to march on Dublin?

This question was particularly apt, for while the south of Ireland had manifested loyalty, it had not been so in the north. The abortive French expedition brought home forcefully to Dublin Castle the massive threat posed by the United Irishmen in Ulster. Already, in September 1796, many of the leaders of the Belfast United Irishmen had been betrayed by an informer, the English merchant William Bird, alias John Smith, and imprisoned, and in November that year large areas of Counties Down and Armagh had been proclaimed under the Insurrection Act. But such measures had had little effect on the progress of the United Irishmen. Arms raids, and murder, had continued unabated. And the countryside—and the Crown forces—became accustomed to the spectacle of communal potato-diggings, designed by the disaffected and rebellious both to display numbers and perhaps to inculcate some elementary military drill. The clamour for a policy of 'counter-terror' had grown, but Camden hitherto had been reluctant to countenance this, perhaps fearful lest London resist such measures. Bantry Bay removed any doubts on this score: severe measures would have to be taken to ensure that if the French did return they would meet little organised support.

Learning the lessons of Bantry Bay

With confirmation of the departure of the French, Camden's Chief Secretary, Thomas Pelham, argued that it was now 'time to reflect on what has passed and, like mariners after a storm, we should lose no time in examining our vessel, stopping all leaks and, I believe, putting in new timbers.' Throughout 1797, and beyond, the lessons Dublin Castle had learnt from the attempted invasion at Bantry Bay were to be put into effect. The Admiralty also took stock of its response to the threatened French invasion.

Royal Navy ships in action in the 1790s

CHANGES IN NAVAL BLOCKADE TACTICS

The Royal Navy, smarting under the remarks directed at it for its failure at Bantry Bay, conducted its own examination into its performance in the crisis, which, perhaps predictably, exonerated itself from all blame. Its failure to intercept the French was excused because 'the state of the information … tho' it had been reported that the enemy had meditated a descent on Ireland, rather led to a belief that their real operations were likely to be directed to the coast of Portugal.'

And yet, for all the public defence of the navy's actions, certain lessons had in fact been learnt about the tactics for blockading enemy ports. These were put into effect, unobtrusively, later in 1797. They would in time—at Trafalgar in 1805—prove spectacularly successful in British naval action against the great French enemy. In the meantime, while there would be further French raids on the Irish coast—for example that by Humbert at Killala in August 1798—as a result of the lessons learnt from the Bantry Bay fiasco the French would never be allowed again to come to Ireland in force.

DISARMING ULSTER, 1797

For twenty years, since the American war and the rise of Volunteering, Ulster, and Presbyterian Belfast, had been the source and centre of Irish radicalism. In the wake of Bantry, Dublin Castle recognised reluctantly that unrest in Ulster was reaching crisis proportions.

On 8 January 1797 Camden revealed to Portland, the Cabinet minister with responsibility for Ireland, that during the emergency provoked by the French at Bantry a large body of troops—nearly ten thousand men—had had to be kept back in Ulster because of the 'very alarming' security situation, particularly in Counties Derry and Antrim (including the town of Belfast). He warned that additional 'severe steps' would have to be taken to crush the conspiracy there.

Portland had earlier balked at the severity of the punishments prescribed in the Insurrection Act (1796), but now, reeling from the near-catastrophe of a French invasion, he pronounced himself in full agreement with these severe measures. 'There is little distinction to be made between indifference and disaffection,' he declared. Within a few months he would suggest to Camden an act of Parliament 'enabling you to depart for a certain time from the established rule of law.' The door was opened to a campaign of official brutality. Ulster was to be dragooned.

Soldiers flogging a prisoner to extract information

The soldier given command of the Ulster campaign was to make his mark in Ireland; for the next two years his name would terrify the Irish as no other since Cromwell. General Gerard Lake, aged fifty-three in 1797, was descended from a former British Secretary of State. He rose through the ranks, serving in Germany and for a time in Ireland before going out to the American war. He saw action at Yorktown before being taken prisoner. Back in England he was appointed an attendant to the Prince of Wales (later King George IV). Throughout the seventeen-nineties, as Lake took part in the French wars, spent a period as governor of Limerick, and then assumed command against the United Irishmen, he was also the sitting MP for the constituency of Aylesbury. Later still he held high command in India. On paper his was a distinguished career; but in Ireland he was to become infamous for the cruelty with which his forces operated.

In the spring of 1797 Camden ordered Lake, in command of a mixed force of Militia, Yeomanry, and Fencibles, to use all methods to disarm Ulster. 'The general has orders from me,' Camden told Portland, 'not to suffer the cause of Justice to be frustrated by the delicacy which might possibly have actuated the magistracy' in implementing the Insurrection Act.

Lake's subordinate commanders set to with a will. 'Laws though ever so strict will not do,' explained General Thomas Knox;

General Gerard Lake

> severe military execution alone will recover the arms from the hands of the rebels ... I look upon Ulster to be a La Vendée [the western region of France whose anti-revolutionary revolt was brutally subjugated by Paris in 1795] ... It will not be brought into subjection but by the means adopted by the republicans in power [in France]—namely spreading devastation through the most disaffected parts.

Throughout the remainder of 1797 a wholesale policy of military terror was instituted in Ulster. House-burnings, floggings and mass arrests were all carried out in order to recover weapons and to cower the populace. In some areas oaths of loyalty were pressed on the inhabitants: nine hundred took the oath in Carrickfergus, County Antrim, and nearly three thousand in Belfast.

Capital convictions too were used to enjoin obedience. At the winter assizes in 1797 some fifty people were sentenced to death. While some were executed, Camden judged it expedient to postpone sentence on the rest, 'from time to time to keep them as hostages for the good behaviour of the neighbourhood.'

Excesses were commonplace; the soldiers were expressly ordered to act without the modest restraint of a civil magistrate present. 'Many are the military outrages which have been committed in the north,' wrote Dr Alexander Haliday, the former Belfast reformer, to Lord Charlemont, former commander of the Volunteers, 'such as inflictions of military punishments on poor people in no way subject to martial law … burglaries, robberies, arsons, murders; and almost every instance passed over without censure or any satisfaction given to the sufferers.'

William Sadler's painting of a Revenue raid gives a glimpse of the terror which the military could inspire in civilians.

Examples are not hard to find. In June 1797 the noted loyalist John Giffard, on duty with his regiment near Newry, County Down, described the devastation wrought by members of the Ancient Britons, a Welsh Fencible regiment, in their search for arms in a small village nearby.

> I was directed by the smoke and flames of burning houses and by the dead bodies of boys and old men slain by the Britons, though no opposition whatever had been given by them and, as I shall answer to Almighty God, I believe a single gun was not fired but by the Britons or Yeomanry. I declare there was nothing to fire at, old men, women and children excepted. From ten to twenty were killed outright, many wounded and eight houses burned.

House-burning as a penalty for possession of arms, or suspicion of concealing arms, was practised extensively. Lord Blayney, dubbed sarcastically the 'Prince of Generals', enthusiastically burnt houses in south Ulster, while in the north-west the activities of Captain Bacon of the Manx Fencibles—soon known as 'Burning Bacon'—were notorious. In one of many instances collected by the noted critic of army tactics Lord Moira, it was reported that at a house-burning near Letterkenny the owner's elderly mother made an attempt to rescue clothing from the fire, whereupon Bacon and his men threw her into the inferno, 'by which she was violently burned.'

There were other refinements. From Moneymore, County Derry, in July 1797 John McCracken wrote to his imprisoned brother, Henry Joy McCracken, telling him of

> the barbarities committed on the innocent country people by the Yeomen and Orangemen. The practice is to hang a man up by the heels with a rope, full of twist, by which means the sufferer whirls around like a bird roasting at the fire during which he is lashed with belts etc. to make him tell where he has concealed arms.

There were instances of rape. The Tipperary Militia, their officers claiming that 'they have authority to waste the country,' were reported to have raped two women in Derry, both of whom subsequently died.

The courts too were pressed into service. William Orr, a young and prosperous

Linen weavers at Banbridge, Co. Down, in the 1790s

Presbyterian farmer of Ballymoney, County Antrim, was indicted for administering the United Irish oath to two soldiers. Under the terms of the Insurrection Act this was a capital offence, and he was the first prisoner to be tried for it. He was found guilty and sentenced to death. Despite many appeals for clemency—and much evidence of irregularities at his trial—Orr was put to death in October 1797. Dublin Castle, in rejecting pleas for mercy, undoubtedly sought to inflict an exemplary punishment in order to overawe the disaffected Dissenters. If so, it badly miscalculated. Orr's popularity, his bearing at his execution and the perceived injustice perpetrated on him served to inspire rather than to terrify the United Irishmen.

Orr claimed, 'If to have loved my country, to have known its wrongs, to have felt the injuries of the persecuted Catholics and to have united with them and all other religious persuasions in the most orderly and least sanguinary means of procuring redress—if these be felonies, I am a felon, but not otherwise.' This defence was widely reported, and a Castle informant wrote that Orr had become the first Presbyterian to be regarded as a Catholic martyr. 'Remember Orr!' would be the war-cry of the United Irishmen of County Antrim in the rebellion. William Drennan, a founding member of the United Irishmen, composed 'The Wake of William Orr':

Write his merits on your mind—

Morals pure and manners kind;

In his head, as on a hill,

Virtue placed her citadel.

Why cut off in palmy youth?

Truth he spoke and acted truth—

'Countrymen, Unite!' he cried,

And died for what his Saviour died.

'It is not to be denied', wrote Camden, 'that government meant to strike terror,' but he justified it by claiming that terror 'had been the policy of the rebellious' and could therefore only be countered by greater terror.

And the army's terror tactics got results. The United Irish network in Ulster was thrown into disarray, large numbers of senior figures were taken up, very large quantities of arms (pikes, muskets and even cannon) were seized, and many thousands—on the United Irishmen's own figures—were terrified out of the movement. Early in 1798 Edward Cooke wrote complacently: 'I believe no part of the King's dominions is more apparently quiet or more evidently flourishing than the north of Ireland.'

MOBILISING LOYALISM, 1797–98

There had been general agreement in Dublin Castle that the one unequivocal success in the Bantry crisis had been the performance of the newly established Irish Yeomanry. Yeomanry corps had mobilised swiftly on receiving news of the French threat, and they had taken over garrison duties from the Militia and regulars. In addition, their officers ('men of three and four thousand pounds a year,' it was noted approvingly) had not felt it to be beneath their dignity to carry out the relatively menial military tasks of carrying expresses or escorting baggage trains. Dublin Castle had certainly had its doubts about the wisdom of an Irish Yeomanry at the time of its formation, for it had feared a repeat of the Volunteer experience of the seventeen-eighties; but the corps' energetic conduct and their enthusiastic loyalty at the moment of danger had dispelled such anxieties.

Moreover, it was clear to the authorities that the formation of the Yeomanry had raised a standard to which loyalists could rally. This was important, related as it was to the

LIST OF SUBSCRIBERS

WHO HAVE ALREADY COME FORWARD

WITH VOLUNTARY CONTRIBUTIONS

IN DEFENCE OF THE COUNTRY.

	L.	s.	D.
M. R. Westropp, for the Royal Cork Volunteers, per Ann. }	600	0	0
Luke O'Shea, per ann. -	60	0	0
Thomas Duggan, per ann. -	11	7	6
Sir Thos. Roberts, Bart. & Co. per ann. }	500	0	0
Sir Jas. Lau. Cotter Bart. & Co. per ann. }	500	0	0
John Anderson, per ann. -	500	0	0
Robert Harding, per ann. -	30	0	0
Messrs. Leslie & Travers, per ann.	500	0	0
Thomas Walker, per ann. -	200	0	0
Isaac Morgan, per ann. -	150	0	0
Pedder & Cotter, per ann. -	200	0	0
John Cuthbert, junr. per ann. -	30	0	0
Anthony Edwards, per ann. -	34	2	6
William Lumley, per ann. -	50	0	0
John Roche jun. (Cove) per ann.	100	0	0
Edmond Roche Kinfelagh -	11	7	6
Richard & William Lane, per ann.	200	0	0
Dominick Lombard -	30	0	0
Alexander Law -	22	15	0
Doctor Meade, per ann. -	20	0	0
Leycester M'Calls & Co. -	300	0	0
J. J. & P. Besnard, per ann. -	20	0	0
Thomas Gibbings -	50	0	0
A. T. Sam Payo -	30	0	0
Edward Hen. Morgan, per ann. -	11	7	6
Samuel Hayman, M.D. -	10	0	0
Henry Osborne, M.D. -	5	13	9
Joseph Rogers, sen. -	50	0	0
Thomas Woodward -	50	0	0
John Forster, per ann. -	50	0	0
Coles & Wood, per ann. -	200	0	0
Daniel Callaghan, per ann. -	100	0	0
Thomas Gibbings, junr. per ann.	20	0	0
John Scraggs, per ann. -	30	0	0
John Good, per ann. -	30	0	0
Robert O'Donnoghue, per ann.	20	0	0
Thomas Pope Heard, per ann. -	11	7	6
Thomas Lindsay, per ann. -	11	7	6
Peter Eason -	11	7	6
Francis Archer White, per ann. -	11	7	6
Jeffery Beasly & Son -	50	0	0
Robert Gibbings, M.D. per ann. -	11	7	6
John Martin, per ann. -	50	0	0
C. M. Clutterbuck, per ann. -	30	0	0
Wilson and Herley, per ann. -	17	1	3
Savage French, per ann. -	455	0	0
George Shea, per ann. -	50	0	0
John Callanan, M. D. -	20	0	0
William Coppinger -	20	0	0
John Cahill, per ann. -	17	1	3
Sir Patrick O'Conor -	22	15	0
Robert M'Clure, per ann. -	11	7	6
William Roche, per ann. -	11	7	6
Paul Maylor, per ann. -	11	7	6
John Steele, per ann. -			
Jas. Harrison, per ann. -	50	0	0
Richard Clear -	11	7	6
John Upsher, per ann. -			
Patrick Goold, per ann. -	20	0	0
Charles Casey, per ann. -	20	0	0
Thomas Waggett, per ann. -	100	0	0
Simon Low, per ann. -	50	0	0
The Right Hon. Lord Viscount Donoughmore }	600	0	0
Dan. Foley, per ann. -	40	0	0
William Phillips, per ann. -	20	0	0
Corporation of the City of Cork -	500	0	0
Hewit, Teulon, & Blunt -	100	0	0
James Morrogh -	50	0	0
John Franklan, per ann. -	11	7	6
John Cole, per ann. -	17	1	3
Chris. Cole, per ann. -	17	1	3
Edward Pope, per ann. -	20	0	0
John Lindsay (Linville) per ann. -	50	0	0
Wm. Maxwell, per ann. -	227	10	0
James Bennett, M. D. per ann. -	10	0	0
Thomas Harding, per ann. -	20	0	0
Thomas Dunscombe, per ann. -	11	7	6
Richard Kellett, for the Loyal Cork Legion, per ann. }	600	0	0
Thomas Westropp, M. D. per ann. -	20	0	0
Robert Richardson, per ann. -	11	7	6
Ephraim White, per ann. -	20	0	0
Shaw & Evanson, per ann. -	40	0	0
Peter Deane, per ann. -	22	15	0
Samuel Hobbs, per ann. -	5	13	9
Warham St. Leger, jun. per ann. -	5	13	9
Wm. Osb. Hamilton, per ann. -	11	7	6
Richard Perry -	50	0	0
John Wily, per ann. -	11	7	6
Montgomery Jennings & Son -	11	7	6
William Kellock, per ann. -	227	10	0
John Sympson, per ann. -	100	0	0
James & William Gregg, per ann. -	20	0	0
John Litchfield, per ann. -	11	7	6
W. Saunders Hallaran, M. D. p. ann. -	10	0	0
Richard Lawton -	22	15	0
Edmond Kenifeck -	40	0	0
Doctor Moylan -	11	7	6
John Connell, per ann. -	11	7	6
Nicholas Geo. Seymour, per ann. -	11	7	6
J. G. Ronan, M. D. -	5	13	9
William Craig -	5	13	9
Wm. Robert Adams, per ann. -	10	0	0
Alexander Brown -	22	15	0
William Cotter -	10	0	0
William Leader -	40	0	0
John Buttle -	2	5	6
W. M. Baker -	22	15	0
Henry Fortescue, per ann. -	22	15	0
Samuel Allin -	11	7	6
Peter Mazeire, per ann. -	20	0	0
William Roberts, per ann. -	10	0	0
A Working Manufacturer -	1	2	9
Sir Samuel Rowland, per ann. -	25		
Lodge No. 1 -			
Wm. Aneran, Limerick, per ann. -	5	13	
J. Stock -			
Margaret Cotter -			

List of loyalist subscribers who contributed to the defeat of the rebellion

experience of British defeat in America. The conventional wisdom was that a prime reason for that defeat was the passive British presumption that American loyalists would come out in support of the Crown. In fact British neglect had allowed the American rebels to intimidate and effectively neutralise latent native loyalism, thus securing an important advantage. This would not be permitted to happen in Ireland.

In the aftermath of Bantry Bay the Orange Order, formed in September 1795, came into its own as an adjunct to the Yeomanry. The order had been set up largely on the initiative of lower-class Protestants in County Armagh, fearful of the growth of Defenderism and concerned at the apparently unchallenged rise of the United Irishmen with their non-denominational message. In 1796 the order had won the approval and patronage of well-to-do Protestant gentry. Some army officers engaged in counter-insurgency duties in Ulster were likewise content to make use of Orangeism, seeing in its strongholds in mid-Ulster a potent barrier to the spread of the United message into west Ulster and north Connacht. Distribution of the *Northern Star*, the primary conduit of the United Irish message, failed to penetrate into or beyond districts where Orangeism took hold. In a real sense, the order held the loyalist line.

General Thomas Knox, on duty in Dungannon, County Tyrone, well recognised the risks in encouraging the Orange Order.

As to the Orangemen, we have rather a difficult card to play. They must not be entirely discountenanced: on the contrary we must in a certain degree uphold them, for with all their licentiousness on them must we rely for the preservation of our lives and fortunes should critical times occur.

And he concluded that 'upon the animosity between the Orangemen and the United Irishmen depends the safety of the centre counties of Ireland.'

The times and their tenor had changed. Dublin Castle throughout 1796 had voiced its deep concern at the Orange Order's activities and had criticised its spread as 'calculated to revive the spirit of religious quarrel and to renew the animosity ... between the Protestant and Catholic sects.' In the aftermath of the French scare at Bantry Bay, however, the Castle pocketed its misgivings about the movement and prepared to turn a blind eye to its excesses. In the end, the Orange Order was indisputably loyal and was therefore to be encouraged.

INFORMERS AND INFORMATION, 1797–98

The harsh measures authorised by Dublin Castle in the wake of the French attempt on Ireland could only be justified by the gravity of the threat facing it from within Ireland. There was, after all, an Irish and a British Parliament, and both Dublin Castle and London were nervous that the severe tactics they advised might not stand up to parliamentary scrutiny. It was therefore vital that the United Irishmen be shown to be treasonably involved with the French, and that their one-time objectives of parliamentary reform and Catholic emancipation be seen to be nothing but a ruse designed to disguise their real aim: an Irish republic.

To that end a Secret Committee of the Irish House of Commons was set up in April 1797. Its purpose was ostensibly to investigate the origins and purpose of the conspiracy in Ireland; but its unstated aim was in fact to provide clear-cut and unambiguous evidence of the deep-seated and extensive nature of the United Irish conspiracy. This the committee duly provided, and its findings were endorsed by a further investigation in 1797 undertaken by the Irish House of Lords.

The information thus published concerning the United Irish treason served two purposes. Firstly, it showed the seriousness of the threat faced by His Majesty's government in Ireland and so validated the terror tactics used to crush the conspiracy.

And, secondly, it did so without resort to show trials, such as had been used earlier in the decade. In these trials the verdict was never certain but the proceedings would surely compromise those informers and agents within the United Irish organisation who were supplying the Castle with crucial information.

Edward Newell, the government informer

From the beginning, the Society of United Irishmen had been under close surveillance. The meetings of the Dublin branch, even though these were entirely open and above board, were reported on regularly by the informer Thomas Collins in the period 1791–94; and in the years after the Society's suppression in 1794 a stream of information from renegade United men poured into Dublin Castle.

Francis Higgins, the 'Sham Squire'

From Saintfield, County Down, Nicholas Mageean, a leading United Irishman, kept the authorities well informed about the society's activities in that county. In Belfast the merchant William Bird, alias Smith, and later Edward John Newell and the bookseller John Hughes passed on copious amounts of gossip and, on occasion, hard information concerning the doings of the United Irishmen of that town. It was a similar story in Dublin, where Francis Higgins, editor of the *Freeman's Journal*, known colloquially as the 'Sham Squire', ran a group of agents on behalf of the Castle and was able to keep his controller, Edward Cooke, in touch with developments in the capital. It was Higgins who recruited Francis Magan, a barrister and United Irishman, to his circle, and it was Magan who ultimately betrayed to Higgins the whereabouts of Edward Fitzgerald.

Beyond Dublin and Belfast the Castle was kept well informed by the likes of Leonard McNally (code-named 'J.W.'), a leading barrister for the United Irishmen, whose legal duties took him all over the country. Regular briefings were also sent in by the postmasters of principal towns, whose duties included opening, copying, resealing and passing on (or not) suspect letters.

Leonard McNally

Similarly, customs officers were useful sources of information in coastal towns, and from all parts came letters from local busybodies eager to report on and denounce their neighbours.

Dublin Castle's knowledge of the United Irish plans up to 1797 was not watertight. Without an appropriate structure for collating, appraising and disseminating intelligence, much valuable information was wasted—as, for example, the reports in late 1796 that a French invasion fleet was preparing at Brest, with Ireland as its destination. But throughout 1797 and beyond there are signs that the Castle was improving its intelligence-gathering and processing capabilities and as a result was able to make a number of important arrests and seizures of arms.

Fortune also favoured the Castle. In October 1797 Samuel Turner, a leading member of the Ulster Directory of the United Irishmen deeply involved in negotiations with the French, revealed all that he knew of the United Irish operations on the Continent to the government. He continued to act as an agent for several years thereafter, though, frustratingly for the Castle, Turner, like many other informers, could not be brought to give evidence in open court.

ROOTING OUT DISAFFECTION IN THE ARMED FORCES, 1797

While Ulster was being 'pacified', loyalists rallied, and an intelligence network devised, the military authorities had also been concerned with putting their own house in order. Their success in combating disaffection among the troops and in sorting out problems of command was to bear significant fruit when the rebellion came.

By common consent, the soldiers had behaved well during the Bantry Bay emergency; but that could be no cause for complacency, for it had long been recognised that there was a problem with disaffection in a large number of regiments, particularly in the Irish Militia, and that if the French had landed in strength the suborned soldiers might have mutinied. Accordingly, throughout 1797 (and after) a close watch was kept on those regiments felt to be at risk. There was a cascade of orders insisting that soldiers wear proper uniform, avoid taverns, and remain in their barracks after retreat.

The British naval mutinies of April and May 1797 at the Nore and Spithead, naval dockyards in eastern and southern England, respectively, and the strong evidence of United Irish involvement in these, reinforced the army's concern at disaffection among the soldiers. Investigations were launched into allegations of disaffection in various regiments, and on foot of these a series of courts-martial was held in the summer of 1797 at army camps throughout Ireland. At places as far apart as Dublin, Bandon, Limerick, and Blaris, near Belfast, men from the Louth, Wexford, Westmeath, Kildare, Leitrim, Galway, Meath, Clare, Kerry, Monaghan and Tipperary Militia and the 5th Dragoon Guards were court-martialled for sedition. About twenty of those convicted were put to death. Many more were given severe floggings and ordered to serve abroad for life.

Perhaps the most significant court-martial was that held at the strategically vital Blaris camp, about ten miles from Belfast. Here four members of the Monaghan Militia were publicly paraded on top of a wagon from Belfast to Blaris, then shot by firing squad. Their deaths severed the links between the disaffected soldiers of Blaris and the United Irishmen of Belfast and appear to have been sufficient to bring other disaffected soldiers back to their duty. Already reeling from Lake's dragonnade, the United Irishmen were forced to realise that they could no longer count on the Militia as some sort of substitute army in case the French did not return.

As if to drive home this message, on the day following these executions men of the Monaghan Militia stormed into Belfast and wrecked the offices and printing press of the *Northern Star*. The paper, founded by Samuel Neilson and so long the loud and energetic voice of the United Irish movement, was never to reopen.

Changes in the military command in Ireland, 1797

The Bantry Bay emergency had exposed the incompetence of the army command in Ireland, and during 1797 steps were taken to bring in effective and efficient generals to command the troops. There was common agreement that there was much negligence and absenteeism among officers—Pelham complained at officers leaving their men on the march south to intercept the French—and Carhampton sent a list of nineteen officers whom he wanted superseded for absenteeism. General Dalrymple, in command at Cork, was elderly and very overweight, and in preparing for his march to Bandon he had allegedly given priority to his personal supply of cayenne pepper and capers. Not surprisingly, his conduct caused murmurings among his subordinates and among observers.

Lord Cornwallis

A local Cork magnate, Lord Longueville, commented in a letter to Dublin Castle that the generals in the Munster area 'are not worth a rap halfpenny,' and he reported that when 'Dalrymple had a fit at Dunmanway and fell off his chair, the people under his command were sorry he recovered.' Dalrymple soon went; so too did General Stewart, who had recently had a stroke and was forced to retire on grounds of ill-health; and General Amherst was got rid of because of 'some very questionable language he was in the habit of.'

Both Stewart and Amherst were pronounced to be 'perfectly useless' by Camden. Others could not be forced out quite so easily, and there still remained a number of 'military exotics' (as John Fitzgibbon, Lord Clare, dubbed them) on the Irish staff. Camden adjudged Carhampton himself to have performed poorly both during and after the emergency at Bantry Bay. In fact Carhampton had never enjoyed the confidence of Dublin Castle. He had drawn unwelcome attention to his tactics in Connacht in 1795 and had only been made commander-in-chief in October 1796 because there was nobody else around. Camden soon began a search for a replacement. 'For all his merit,' noted Camden, 'there is certainly a degree of indiscretion in his character that makes him unfit for the chief commands of the army in times so delicate as the present and the military certainly do not place great confidence in him.'

Ironically, the attempted invasion by the French had made a command in Ireland more attractive to ambitious career officers, for the country was now a theatre of war, where reputation, honour and glory could be won: it could be an Italy in the west for some hungry British general. Lord Cornwallis, a veteran of America and India, was approached, but he declined the command; and it was General Ralph Abercromby—according to Henry Dundas, minister of war, 'one of the best if not on the whole the very best officers in the King's service'—who took up the challenge in October 1797. It was reported that 'the army rejoice at the change.' Its joy was not to last.

The road to rebellion, January 1797 to May 1798

As Ulster was scoured for arms, the United Irishmen waited and kept their heads down. A firm order went out that they were not to engage the King's forces in combat but were instead to hold their fire and bide their time. They were not to draw attention to themselves, lest they provoke an even greater onslaught than that already being visited on them. Some were even encouraged to take the oath of allegiance prescribed under the Insurrection Act so as to lull government suspicions.

Central to United Irish thinking at this time was the policy that the organisation must remain intact to welcome its French allies when they would return. However, as the months passed and the arrests, deportations and arms seizures multiplied, divisions—always latent—began to appear within the ranks, north and south, concerning the wisdom of this policy of inaction.

Some northern United Irishmen, particularly among the rank and file, began to demand a military response to the Castle's tactics. They argued that waiting for the French was proving too costly: their organisation was

Samuel Neilson

being dismantled piecemeal and soon would be able to offer no support to their allies when they landed. Further, they maintained that the surest way to hasten the arrival of the French was to stage an insurrection unilaterally, for the Directory would not pass up that opportunity of striking at Britain. More pragmatically, they declared it was better to die fighting than to sheepishly await their fate at the hands of the Yeomen.

Jemmy Hope, weaver and United Irishman

Years later, the weaver and United Irish campaigner Jemmy Hope recalled bitterly that 'the people were in daily expectation of being called to the field by their leaders, an intention as it appeared afterwards, which the leaders had little intention of putting into execution.' The fact was that other United Irishmen, particularly in the Leinster Executive—Thomas Addis Emmet, William MacNeven, and Richard McCormick—continued to counsel caution, for they were well aware that their organisation was very imperfectly established outside Ulster and Dublin. The lack of response in Munster to the 'French in the Bay' in December 1796 had shown that much organising had to be undertaken in that area. In any case, Emmet was fearful lest an insurrection undertaken without the guidance, discipline and weaponry to be provided by the French would quickly collapse in confusion or, worse, degenerate into a sectarian bloodbath.

In this debate the voice of those who argued for delay prevailed—at least for the time being. New envoys had been sent to France in the middle of 1797 urging action, and early in 1798 word arrived that the French expected to be in Ireland in the spring; the decision was to await their arrival. A military committee was formed to co-ordinate and plan the United Irish strategy, and in the meantime the United Irishmen sought to extend their organisation beyond Ulster.

Dublin Castle's determination to root out disloyalty in Ulster, and its despatch of a large army for that purpose, had the unintentional side effect of allowing the United Irishmen to organise elsewhere in relative secrecy. Counties Westmeath and Meath were already centres of Defenderism; there the United men blended with the Defenders. King's County (Offaly), with its Defender lodges, was also soon infiltrated by the United Irishmen. By the end of the year, largely through the efforts of emissaries from Ulster such as William Putnam McCabe, Samuel Neilson, and Jemmy Hope, the organisation had spread into Counties Wicklow, Carlow, Kildare, Kilkenny, Tipperary, Cork, and finally Wexford.

The Wexford organisation stood apart in one important respect: only here was United Irish penetration undertaken with anything approaching secrecy. This was to be significant for the future. Elsewhere, the spread of the United Irish conspiracy was accompanied by arms raids, agrarian outrages, and selective assassination. By March 1798 magistrates had been murdered in Kildare, Queen's County (Laois), Tipperary, and Cork. Informers were everywhere at risk. From Waterford came a report of the death of a suspected informer; his assailants, 'not content with murdering the informer himself, murdered his wife and daughter; and that nothing alive should be left in the house, the dog that belonged to the family was killed also.'

On all sides, the descent into political violence gave rise to an amount of score-settling in old disputes over land, rent, or tithes. The political atmosphere grew sectarian and poisonous. Cynically, the United Irishmen made use of the 'Orange card' to win recruits, even going as far as to circulate bogus bloodcurdling Orange oaths advocating the massacre of Catholics. One such oath found in Nenagh, County Tipperary, in November 1797 ran:

William Pitt the Younger, the Prime Minister

I, A.B., swear that I will be true to the King and government and that I will exterminate all the Catholics in Ireland.

The oaths were false, but plausible to many. Thousands of Catholics had been driven from their homes in south Ulster, especially County Armagh, in 1796 and 1797, and as they migrated south and west they brought with them a desire for revenge and a fear of Orangeism. Curiously, those areas where the Orange Order was least in evidence were precisely the places most in terror of it.

As rumours of a sectarian bloodbath circulated freely, panic spread. There were reports that the population of entire villages had taken to sleeping out of doors in the belief that they stood a better chance of survival there. Magistrates who were 'active' (i.e. ruthless), frequently Church of Ireland ministers or Yeomanry officers—or both— played their part in creating a climate of terror. Rigged trials dispensed a partisan justice. From the Maryborough (Port Laoise) assizes in early 1798 the government informer Leonard McNally related the scandalous proceedings by which thirteen Defenders were convicted of capital offences.

THE

O A T H

To be miniftred unto every FREEMAN of the CITY of *DUBLIN*.

YOU fhall fwear, That you fhall be good and true to our Sovereign Lord KING *GEORGE* the Third, and to the Heirs of our faid Sovereign Lord the KING: Obeyfant and Obedient you fhall be to the MAYOR and Minifters of this City. The Franchifes and Cuftoms thereof you fhall maintain, and this City keep harmlefs, in *that* that in you is: You fhall be contributary to all Manner of Charges within this City, as Summons, Watches, Contributions, Tafks, Tallages, Lot, and Scot, and all other Charges bearing you Part as a Freeman ought to do: You fhall colour no foreign Goods, whereby the KING or this City might lofe their Cuftoms or Advantages. You fhall know no Foreigner to buy or fell any Merchandizes with any other Foreigner within this City, or Franchiles thereof, but you fhall warn the MAYOR thereof: You fhall take no Apprentice but if he be freeborn, that is to fay, no Bondfman's Son, and for no lefs Term than for feven Years; within the firft Year you fhall caufe him to be inrolled, and at his Term's End you fhall make him Free of this City, if he have well and truly ferved you: You fhall alfo keep the KING'S Peace in your own Perfon, and fhall always, whilft you are able and in your Power, keep a good Mufket, Carbine or Fufee, in good, clean and fufficient Order: You fhall know no Gatherings, Conventicles, nor Confpiracies, made againft his Majefty's Peace, but you fhall warn the MAYOR thereof, or let it to your Power: You fhall not be free Baker, Butcher or Fifher, without you pay Cuftom; and whatfoever Office that you be lawfully called unto, within the faid Franchiles, you fhall not refufe. All thefe Points and Articles you fhall well and truly keep according to the Laws and Cuftoms of this City, to your Power. So GOD you help, and by the holy Contents of this Book.

GOD fave the KING.

A loyalty oath

The defences set up by the prisoners were treated too often with inattention, laughter and contempt, everything against them received as truth. In some cases the judge's authority could scarcely preserve the decorum necessary to a court of justice and this conduct was severely felt and bitterly complained of by the lower people to those in whom they could confide ... Some gentlemen of fortune wore Orange ribbands and some barristers sported Orange rings with emblems. Such ensigns of enmity, I assure you, are not conducive to reconciliation.

By early 1798 Ireland was a place of great fear. The United Irish movement was still spreading. Increasingly there were reports of preparations for an uprising. A French landing was thought imminent. Rumours abounded of another massacre on the scale of that perpetrated in 1641. Loyalists everywhere clamoured for martial law to be proclaimed throughout Ireland and, above all, for the armed forces to be given a free hand everywhere.

To loyalist fury, the commander-in-chief, General Abercromby, resisted these demands. Appalled by the indiscipline of the forces he commanded, he was not prepared to turn them loose on the disaffected. In March 1798, however, he was forced to resign.

THE ABERCROMBY AFFAIR, 1797–98

On his appointment in October 1797 Sir Ralph Abercromby had had some previous experience of Ireland and the Irish, and he had already formed certain fairly conventional views on the country and its inhabitants. The Irish people were fine if they were treated well; they made good soldiers if well led; the Irish gentry were contemptible. These earlier impressions were confirmed on his arrival in Ireland, and from the beginning the new commander-in-chief was on a collision course with the Castle.

Abercromby was convinced that the threat of invasion from France must take precedence over the danger (much exaggerated, in his opinion) of domestic insurrection, and he therefore decided to concentrate his troops in large numbers, and to enforce discipline among them. Moreover, he determined to shift the responsibility for law and

A United Irish device showing an Irish harp surmounted by a Phrygian cap, a symbol of the French Revolution

order away from the army and onto the Yeomanry and the local gentry. The lack of discipline among the soldiers greatly alarmed him. Reports of murder, rape, house-burning, attacks on civilians and pillaging reached him constantly; 'within these twelve months,' he told his son, 'every crime, every cruelty that could be committed by Cossacks or Calmucks has been transacted here.'

Neither Abercromby's criticisms nor his remedies were relished by Camden or his advisers, his 'cabinet' of mostly Irish office-holders that met regularly to review security policy. For a number of years they had treated the country as being in a state of smothered, if not actual, rebellion, and they had deployed their forces accordingly. Abercromby now dismissed their fears as exaggerated, and he quickly shut himself off from them.

If Abercromby had kept his remarks internal to the army, a collision between him and the Castle's advisers might have been avoided; but on 26 February 1798, following the rape by two officers of a witness to a murder, he issued his notorious 'General Orders' in which he denounced the Irish forces as being in a state of licentiousness 'which must render it formidable to everyone but the enemy.' These strictures on the forces he commanded raised a furore, and within a few weeks Abercromby had resigned, claiming that he had lost the confidence of Camden. Officially Camden made great efforts to persuade him to stay on, but by the end of March, and in confidence to the Prime Minister, William Pitt, he reported that Abercromby's position had become untenable. In any case, Camden felt that Abercromby was guilty of an apparently leisurely pursuit of subversives and their weapons.

On 14 March 1798, as the furore over his General Orders was just beginning, Abercromby had been formally ordered to disarm Kildare, Queen's County (Laois), and King's County (Offaly). However, Abercromby determined that, unlike Lake's campaign in Ulster, this would be no dragonnade. He immediately opened his campaign by issuing a series of commands to his men to maintain strict discipline, to exercise the greatest moderation, and not to go off without an officer. He then sent out thousands of printed proclamations giving the disaffected ten days' notice to bring in their arms. Failure would mean 'free quarters'—the billeting of troops among the terrified populace themselves. This delay was widely criticised. 'There is very general discontent expressed at Abercromby's method of proceeding,' wrote one Castle supporter; and Lord Clifden, on duty with his regiment in Kilkenny, exploded: 'Is Abercrombie turned Jacobin or old woman? I hear the latter!' Moreover, the commander's threat of free quarters was ridiculed as calculated to hurt the well-to-do more than the disaffected, who were poor and had little to lose. In the event, only a small quantity of arms and almost no pikes were recovered. Camden pronounced himself entirely dissatisfied with Abercromby's conduct. He had to go.

A new commander-in-chief was sought; and General Gerard Lake, then dragooning Ulster, was chosen. Camden had not wanted him, because he felt Lake lacked judgment; but Pitt was in a bullish mood. Lake was 'brave, active and, I believe, popular,' he claimed. He argued that Lake's appointment would constitute the best answer to Abercromby's strictures. The terror tactics adopted by Lake in Ulster were now to be extended throughout the country.

MILITARY OPERATIONS ON THE EVE OF THE REBELLION

Three years earlier the recall of Fitzwilliam, the Viceroy, had meant an end to political concessions. Now the resignation of General Abercromby had a similar impact on the Castle's military policy. Abercromby's departure signalled the adoption of the draconian measures favoured—indeed clamoured for—by Camden's Irish 'cabinet'. 'If we treat rebellion as rebellion, we are safe,' wrote Edward Cooke in March 1798; and Lord Clifden reported that he had got Pitt to agree that 'terror could only be repressed by stronger terror.'

On 30 March all Ireland was formally proclaimed under the Insurrection Act. As far as Dublin Castle was concerned, the rebellion had begun. The following day Pitt indicated the strategy now to be pursued: Camden was told 'to make a speedy and (as far as circumstances will admit) a well-concerted effort for crushing the rebellion by the most vigorous military exertions in all the disturbed provinces.' Moreover, he was not to concern himself unduly with army discipline. In his turn, General Lake was ordered to abandon free quarters as a weapon and to 'adopt such other vigorous and effectual measures for enforcing the speedy surrender of arms.'

Flogging, house-burning and torture were now employed on a large scale. 'We are out every day foraging [for arms] and burning the houses of known rebels,' wrote Lord Clifden from Kilkenny in early May. He pointed out that he had not hesitated to burn the

Military terror was freely employed in both town and countryside in the attempt to cow the population and to discover hidden arms deposits.

homes of his own tenantry. From Queen's County the young army officer Lord Wycombe remarked jocularly that he and his men had been involved in 'a little torture as well as robbery' but then, more sombrely, confessed that his men 'are perpetually doing acts under the sanction of the Lord Lieutenant and Privy Councils for which a French soldier in an invading army would be shot.'

Sir Benjamin Chapman, a member of the Irish Parliament, later recalled to his correspondent Lord Shelburne how he had gone to a cold-plate dinner at a friend's house some five miles distant from Trim, County Meath.

What a dessert had we to our frugal repast! The sudden and shocking exhibition from our windows of the perspective of a conflagration of the surrounding mansions, of farmers and peasants flying for shelter in all directions and unexpectedly involved in this dreadful calamity; a regiment of Scotch Fencibles enjoyed this savage triumph and fired upon the fugitives while thirty wretched houses ... with every sort

of provision, rustic furniture and implements of husbandry were all consumed by the merciless flames before our eyes. I could hear no reason save that a robbery had been attempted without success a few days before on a gentleman in that vicinage.

Flogging especially was employed to elicit confessions and to force the prisoner to divulge where arms were concealed. Even those most in favour of 'firmness', such as Lord Shannon (who recommended shooting ten hostages for every loyalist casualty), conceded that 'the cat is laid on with uncommon severity'; but against that it was acknowledged that 'by proper flagellation quantities of arms have been given up.'

The Bishop of Killaloe, on the Clare-Tipperary border, claimed that 1,500 pikes had been seized in his area but that now Major Wilford was 'determined to try what flogging may do' to uncover more. From County Limerick, John Massey claimed that 'a power of whipping those fellows [suspects] into confession is absolutely necessary,' house-burning on its own not being sufficient.

From County Wicklow the Quaker Mary Leadbeater confided to her journal the horrors she witnessed in her village of Ballitore.

> To the Tyrone Militia [the regular garrison] were now added the Suffolk Fencibles. And the Ancient Britons, dressed in blue with much silver lace—a very pretty dress—came from Athy, seized the smiths' tools to prevent them from making pikes, and made prisoners of the smiths themselves. I could not see without emotion poor Owen Finn and his brother, handcuffed and weeping as they walked after the car containing those implements of industry which had enabled them to provide comfortably for the family. Several of them were whipped publicly to extort confessions about the pikes. The torture was excessive and the victims were long in recovering; and in almost every case it was applied fruitlessly ... The village once so peaceful exhibited a scene of tumult and dismay, and the air rang with the shrieks of the sufferers and the lamentations of those who beheld them suffer.

In County Tipperary the high sheriff, Thomas Judkin Fitzgerald, soon became notorious for his unsparing use of the 'cat'. A special Indemnity Act had to be passed after the rebellion to protect him from those he had tormented.

Lord Edward Fitzgerald

As the military onslaught mounted throughout April and May, the United Irishmen prepared to complete their plans for a rising, if need be without their French allies. However, the terror unleashed by the armed forces in their campaigns of early 1798 had excited furious resentment everywhere. A poisonous rancour bubbled to the surface of Irish society, and revenge jostled with pride and mingled with savage fury to produce the conflagration that overswept the land in late May.

UNITED IRISH PREPARATIONS—AND ARRESTS

By early 1798 the United Irishmen were actively preparing for an insurrection, with or without the French. The voices of those who argued that they could not indefinitely await the arrival of the French were becoming dominant. Both Arthur O'Connor and Edward Fitzgerald, who formerly had been reluctant to move without their overseas allies, now turned ardent advocates for such a course.

By 1797 Fitzgerald had become the talismanic personality among the United Irishmen. Born to the premier family of the Anglo-Irish nobility, the Dukes of Leinster, he

The brothers John (above) and Henry (left) Sheares, radical lawyers and United Irishmen

should have had the effortlessly rising career of an Ascendancy leader. His early years as a British army officer in America, where he fought bravely for King and Empire, fitted perfectly. But the age of revolution had captivated him, and Fitzgerald transformed himself into an ardent revolutionary—a hero to the Dublin working people and radicals, a class traitor and bitter enemy to the conservatives.

France had much to do with it. Fitzgerald's mother, determined that the children should have good French tutelage, enquired about the possibility of bringing Jean-

Leinster House in Dublin, town house of the Duke of Leinster

Jacques Rousseau himself to Frescati House, Blackrock, to educate the children. Instead she brought them to France, where Edward grew up Francophone and Francophile. And though he fought the French in America (where he was made an honorary chief by the Iroquois), the revolution in 1789 changed everything. He cropped his hair in the French revolutionary style, thus becoming one of the first of those the Irish came to know as 'Croppies'. He renounced his aristocratic title in favour of that of Citizen. He married a Catholic, Pamela, reputed to be the daughter of Philippe Égalité, Duke of Orléans, one of the French revolutionary leaders. He returned to Ireland convinced that only revolution could bring about justice and equality in his own country.

In Dublin, Fitzgerald did away with his horse and carriage, walking the streets among the ordinary people with his tricoloured French cravat and cropped hair. In the theatre he hissed the playing of 'God Save the King' and demanded the United Irish version, 'God Save the Rights of Man', instead. The Ascendancy were outraged; the people adored him. But behind the glamour and the image was a natural leader who knew military action. To the United Irishmen he was a huge asset, to the Castle an increasingly marked man.

According to Fitzgerald's calculations there were in the region of 280,000 armed United Irishmen in the country, a force sufficient to wrest control from Dublin Castle and hold the country until their French allies landed. Those who continued to advise delay lost ground. Thomas Addis Emmet just barely prevailed on his colleagues in the Leinster Directory to wait a few more weeks, arguing that the French invasion could not be much longer. However, the tide was turning decisively in favour of action. Another advocate of caution, Richard McCormick, realising that his side had lost the debate, fled Ireland, not to return till after the rebellion.

The informer Thomas Reynolds

Through its agents and informers the Castle was quite well briefed on the debate within the leadership. Nicholas Mageean from Saintfield, County Down, sent in a stream of information relating to the United Irishmen in their strongest county, and Leonard McNally kept the Castle posted on what was going on in Dublin. Moreover, information was coming from Hamburg from Samuel Turner, the leading member of the Ulster Directory who had been deeply involved in negotiations with the French. This was priceless in helping Edward Cooke to fit the pieces of the jigsaw together.

But there were still gaps in Dublin Castle's knowledge. Much of its information would not stand up in court, and few of its agents were prepared to go into the witness box. Moreover, London was afraid that a premature seizure of the leaders might

GOVERNMENT BULLETIN.

DUBLIN CASTLE, 15th MY, 1798.

The Lord Lieutenant and Privy Council of Ireland have issued a proclamation declaring that they have received information upon oath, that Lord EDWARD FITZGERALD has been guilty of high treason, and offer a reward of £1000 sterling, to any person who shall discover, apprehend, or commit him to prison.

An unexpected event has taken place in this city; namely, a cession made by the Corporation for the improvement of Dublin Harbour, of their property in the Pigeon-house Dock, and the newly-constructed hotel, to Government, for the purpose of a place of arms and military post, if not for ever, at least during the present war. The part allotted for this place of arms is, we hear, to be insulated by strong redoubts, mounted with cannon.

Dublin, May 20th,

Yesterday evening information having been given of the place in which Lord Edward Fitzgerald had concealed himself, Mr. Justice Swan, Major Sirr, and Captain Ryan, with a small guard, went in two coaches to the house of one Murphy, a feather merchant, in Thomas-street. Major Sirr instantly proceeded to plant sentinels on the different doors of the house; Mr. Swan and Captain Ryan rushed in, and ran up to a room two pair of stairs backwards. Mr. Swan, having first reached the door, opened it, and told Lord Edward, who lay upon a bed in his dressing-gown and breeches, that he had a warrant against him; adding, " You know me, my Lord, and I know you : it will be in vain to resist." They approched each other : his Lordship, on their meeting, stabbed Mr. Swan, with a dagger; the latter fired : they struggled : Lord Edward, in the struggle, wounded him a second time in the back; the dagger glanced upon his ribs : Mr. Swan straggered back, crying out that he was killed. Captain Ryan by this time arrived, and rushed in : he presented a pocket pistol , it missed fire, he drew a sword from his stick, drew double upon the body of Lord Edward, the latter staggered, and fell backwards upon the bed, Captain Ryan threw himself upon him, Lord Edward plunged the dagger into Captain Ryan's side, they grappled with each other, Captain Ryan endeavouring to wrest the dagger. Lord Edward stabbing him, and eluding his grasp. The whole business was so instantaneous, that Major Sirr had only time to reach the room-door, from hearing the discharge of the first shot, which had alarmed him, he rushed in, saw Captain Ryan and Lord Edward struggling and entwined upon the floor, Major Sirr discharged a pistol, and wounded Lord Edward in the shoulder, the latter then cried out for mercy, and was secured. Some of Captain Ryan's wounds are of the most alarming nature, he has received no less than 14 stabs in different parts of his body, of these, one is peculiarly alarming, it is situate under his left ribs, and, though there is every reason to hope that the intestines are uninjured, we cannot venture to pronounce him out of danger. Mr. Swan's wounds are not so serious, they are likely soon to heal, Lord Edward was sent from the Castle, after a short examination, to Newgate, his wounds are supposed to be but slight.

DUBLIN : Printed by GEORGE GRIERSON, Printer to the King's Most Excellent Majesty.

A contemporary account of the arrest of Lord Edward Fitzgerald

The capture of Lord Edward Fitzgerald. This colour illustration is taken from the nationalist paper Young Ireland *in 1885.*

endanger its intelligence network in France. For these reasons the Castle was at first reluctant to strike against the leadership. Then in February, just as the United Irishmen's plans were being completed, Dublin Castle received the break it needed.

Thomas Reynolds was a member of the Leinster Directory, a friend of Fitzgerald and Tone's brother-in-law. Under Fitzgerald's auspices he had been promoted up the ranks in the organisation. Now he decided to tell what he knew to the authorities.

On 12 March, as a result of Reynolds's information, almost the entire leadership of the Leinster Directory was arrested in the home of Oliver Bond. The Castle followed these arrests with the proclamation of martial law throughout Ireland on 30 March. A manhunt was launched for the few United leaders who had escaped the swoop. Foremost among these was Fitzgerald. With a reward of a thousand pounds on his head, he remained at large in Dublin until 19 May; then his hiding-place was revealed to Dublin Castle by Francis Higgins. He was seized after a desperate struggle in which one man died and he himself was seriously wounded.

Fitzgerald's capture was another huge setback to the United Irishmen, for it was believed that his name on its own was worth an army, and no-one could doubt his determination. Alone among the United Irish leadership he had had a military career; he had seen active service in America, where he had been wounded in battle. He was almost certainly the author of the United Irish military strategy. This called for a rising on the night of 23 May—to be signalled by the burning of the mail coaches to Belfast, Cork, Limerick, and Athlone—and Fitzgerald himself was to lead the assault on the capital. There would be other risings to the north (Counties Antrim and Down), west (Kildare and Carlow), and south (Wexford and Wicklow), and these would prevent the Crown forces mobilising against the rebels in Dublin; the rapid arrival of the French would complete the rebels' triumph. The capture of Fitzgerald threw this plan into disarray.

Moreover, because Fitzgerald had been captured alive, and because his importance to the United Irishmen was well recognised, the Castle authorities fully expected an attempt

The Battle of the Pyramids, 1798. The French, who might have been in Ireland, were in fact gaining their victories in the eastern Mediterranean.

A more contemporary drawing of the capture of Lord Edward Fitzgerald, dating from 1811

at his rescue. All available forces were therefore called out and all roads into, out of and within the capital closely watched. A strict curfew was imposed in the city, and it was reported that 'scarce a cat could steal into this large metropolis at night' because of the ring of troops—'so close … that they can almost converse with each other'—drawn up around likely targets. If the United Irishmen planned to strike on 23 May, Fitzgerald's capture on 19 May had deprived them of the advantage of surprise.

Further disaster struck a day after Fitzgerald's capture. Following the swoop on Bond's house, the general leadership of the movement had passed to Henry and John Sheares, long-time radicals from Cork; but, fatally, they had taken Captain John Armstrong of the King's County Militia into their confidence, believing him to be a sympathiser. They had questioned him about the disposition of the troops at Loughlinstown, and Armstrong had immediately informed his commanding officer of what was afoot. The brothers were placed under close surveillance and were arrested the day after Fitzgerald's capture. They were later hanged.

With Fitzgerald in Newgate prison, mortally wounded, the Sheares brothers under close arrest, the Castle authorities fully alerted and most of the other first-rank leaders in jail or else fled the country, hopes for a successful rising cannot have been high. Even the perennially suspicious spymaster Edward Cooke relaxed his guard: he confided to a colleague that he was warily confident that insurrection had been abandoned for the time being. Everything now appeared to depend on the French. Would they come?

THE UNITED IRISHMEN AND FRANCE, 1797–98

Despite the setback at Bantry Bay, the United Irishmen in France, Tone prominent among them, had still been confident that another expedition would be fitted out for Ireland. This, however, could not take place for some time. Indeed the mere rumour of a fast return to Ireland had prompted a threat of mutiny from both soldiers and sailors at the port of Brest, and any such idea was quickly given up. Tone had been assured that the Directory had merely postponed, not abandoned, a further descent on Ireland.

In May 1797 the Directory had ordered its ally the Batavian Republic (i.e. the Netherlands) to undertake an expedition to Ireland, involving some fifteen thousand troops and making use of the Dutch fleet in the Texel. Tone and the other United Irishmen who joined him in Holland looked forward with eager anticipation to a speedy voyage to Ireland; but in the event they met with further frustration, for the winds refused to turn and the fleet was unable to sail. A mutiny of the British North Sea fleet meant that there was, unusually, a real chance of an unopposed crossing to Ireland; but the delay forced by the weather meant that the opportunity afforded to the Dutch warships could not be availed of. As July turned to August and still the winds remained contrary, the window of opportunity was firmly shut. In September came the crushing news of Hoche's death from consumption, and the expedition was finally abandoned.

In December 1797, in another effort to get things moving again, Tone went back to Paris. There he had a number of meetings with Napoléon Bonaparte, the new power in France. Bonaparte listened politely while Tone plied him with maps and memorandums on Ireland (some dating from 1795), but he remained noncommittal about any Irish adventures. An 'Armée d'Angleterre' had indeed been formed, and, though Tone was given a staff post as adjutant-general, the plan called for an attack on England, not on Ireland.

A further setback for Irish hopes was the disgrace of Carnot, now accused of being—

of all things—a royalist and consequently forced to flee France. With the death of Hoche and the removal of Carnot (and the shadow that lay on those hitherto associated with them), the United Irish mission to France by early 1798 had all but come to an end.

The French army earmarked to invade England continued to wait impatiently at the Channel ports. But a full-scale invasion of England was never really on. Bonaparte knew that command of the sea was necessary before a crossing could be ventured, and that was effectively out of the question. In any case he was a Corsican, whose heart had long been set on a campaign in Egypt, preparatory perhaps to an onslaught on India. And so, as Edward Fitzgerald lay wounded and dying in Dublin and the burning of the mail coaches signalled the outbreak of the Irish insurrection, Bonaparte and his mighty army were afloat in the Mediterranean, but heading for Egypt, not Ireland. The rebellion in Ireland was doomed from the beginning; no rebellion in the Atlantic world for two hundred years had succeeded without generous foreign assistance. If the United Irishmen rose in rebellion they would do so on their own.

DUBLIN CASTLE AND THE REBELLION

It seems clear that Dublin Castle welcomed the prospect of the secret conspiracy finally becoming an open contest. It was convinced that some 300,000 United Irishmen and Defenders remained sworn in to the conspiracy; how else could these be crushed save in open confrontation? As early as May 1797 Camden had told Portland: 'I shall not lament the attempt at insurrection. It will enable us to act with effect.' A year later, when news arrived of the seizure of the mail coaches on the night of 23/24 May, swiftly followed by reports of open fighting in County Kildare and elsewhere, the first reaction of Dublin Castle was far from alarmist. This rebellion, wrote Cooke, is 'really the salvation of the country. If you look to the accounts that 200,000 are sworn in a conspiracy, how would that conspiracy be cleared without a burst?'

A former Lord Lieutenant, Westmorland, agreed. 'I am glad the explosion has burst,' he told the Archbishop of Cashel, 'and trust you will soon be restored to quiet.' He concluded, however, that the 'seditious spirit was become so universal' that 'considerable examples' would have to be made.

Camden, however, now struck a cautionary note, for the clamour for 'examples' caused him alarm. Already, in March 1798, he had drawn attention to the emergence of 'the most extravagant party prejudices ... calling the present conspiracy a Popish plot,' and within a few days of the outbreak of the rebellion he would report that 'savage cruelties ... party and religious prejudice has literally made the Protestant part of the country mad.' Ominously, he added, 'The army partake of the fury. It is scarcely possible to restrain the violence of our immediate friends and advisors within bounds. They are prepared for extirpation ...'

The old Houses of Parliament in London

3

THE RISING

In the circumstances, it was a cause for wonder that the United Irishmen should have been in a position to stage any sort of insurrection in May 1798. Two years of relentless harrying by government forces had taken their toll on membership, leadership, and morale. The arrest of Edward Fitzgerald and of the Sheares brothers, together with the seizure of some papers in their possession, had alerted the Castle to the imminent danger it faced, and the capital was quickly made secure.

By May 1798 the prospect of French help was forlorn, as Bonaparte fixed his gaze on Egypt and directed his forces thither; and that substitute army of disaffected and suborned Irish soldiers that the United Irishmen had counted on

NOTICE.

LIEUTENANT GENERAL LAKE, commanding His Majesty's Forces in this Kingdom, having received from His EXCELLENCY the Lord LIEUTENANT full Powers to PUT DOWN THE REBELLION, and to punish REBELS in the most summary Manner, according to Martial Law, does hereby give Notice to all his Majesty's Subjects, that he is determined to exert the Powers entrusted to him in the most vigorous Manner, for the immediate Suppression of the same; and that all Persons acting in the present Rebellion, or in any wise aiding or assisting therein, will be treated by him as Rebels, and punished accordingly.

And LIEUTENANT GENERAL LAKE hereby requires all the Inhabitants of the City of DUBLIN, (the great Officers of State, Members of the Houses of Parliament, Privy Counsellors, Magistrates, and Military Persons in Uniform excepted) to remain within their respective Dwellings from NINE o'Clock at Night till FIVE in the Morning, under Pain of Punishment.

By Order of LIEUTENANT GENERAL LAKE,
Commanding His Majesty's Forces in this Kingdom,

G. HEWETT, Adjutant-General.

Dublin, Adjutant General's Office,
24th May, 1798.

Lake's proclamation on the outbreak of the rebellion

had signally failed to materialise. As a result of the early and very disruptive arrests, and especially the failure of Dublin to rise, the rebellion when it came was distinguished by a lack of co-ordination and a lack of focus. Moreover, it tended to be conducted by local leaders with local reputations rather than by the better-known principals, now dead or in prison.

Dublin and the surrounding counties, 23–29 May

At ten o'clock on the night of 24 May 1798, Camden, on receiving the news of open rebellion, wrote excitedly to the Home Secretary in London. 'Martial law is established—the sword is drawn—I have kept it within the scabbard as long as possible—it must not be returned until this most alarming conspiracy is put down.' Earlier that morning the rebels in County Kildare launched attacks on Prosperous, Naas, Clane, Rathangan, and Kilcullen bridge. At Prosperous there was a minor rebel victory. A night attack on the village was led by Dr Esmonde—a Yeomanry officer—and the garrison of Ancient Britons and City of Cork Militia was taken by surprise. Many were burnt to death when their barracks were set on fire. Captain Richard Swayne of the Cork Militia, notorious for his pitch-capping of suspects, was shot, piked and trampled under a horse's

Captain Richard Swayne of the Cork Militia, the notorious pitch-capper, who died at Prosperous, Co. Kildare

hooves and his body burnt in a tar barrel. Some forty of his comrades also perished.

At Naas, Lord Gosford of the Armagh Militia, in charge of the defence, reported that the rebels were led by Michael Reynolds, 'whose house we burned some days ago.' Gosford wrote that after a battle lasting about an hour the rebels broke and fled. About 130 of them were killed, mostly as they fled (though Reynolds himself escaped to the

Wicklow Mountains). In addition, several hundred prisoners were taken, and 'three men with green cockades … were hanged in the public street.' The military casualties were six dead and twelve wounded.

The proportion of rebel dead to government casualties was even greater elsewhere. On 24 May, General Lake had issued the order to his commanders to 'take no prisoners,' and a day later General Sir Ralph Dundas, following an engagement in Kilcullen, reported 'about one hundred and thirty [rebel] dead—no prisoners.' An earlier assault by Dundas's cavalry on a rebel position in a churchyard had been repulsed with twenty-three casualties: the pike assaults proved unexpectedly effective against trained cavalry. This time Dundas reported that there were no casualties on the government side—killed, wounded, or missing.

Although not a contemporary illustration, this painting of the Ancient Britons' cavalry charging a United Irish position conveys the drama of the battle scenes as well as a racist stereotype of the rebels.

Over the next few days, 24–29 May, rebellion erupted elsewhere, in Counties Wicklow, Carlow, Kildare and Meath and in the immediate environs of Dublin itself; but everywhere the rebels were rebuffed, usually after sustaining horrendous casualties and sometimes after an initial success. Rebels in arms were reported at Rathfarnham,

Tallaght, Lucan, Lusk, Dunboyne, Barrettstown, Ballymore Eustace, Baltinglass, Narraghmore, Ballitore, Carlow, and Rathangan. At each of these places furious skirmishes or small-scale battles took place. At Barrettstown a hundred rebels were reported dead; there were no military casualties. At Monasterevin some 1,300 rebels were driven off after a battle in which they lost over sixty men, as against five dead on the government side.

A captured rebel

At Carlow perhaps three hundred rebels died in a failed attack on the town; advancing confidently up the main street, they were met with withering cannon fire. Those who were not instantly cut down were pursued as they fled. An eye-witness, William Farrell of Carlow, recorded:

> The soldiers opened on them a most tremendous fire of musketry. The rebels flew like frightened birds. Some forced in the doors of thatched cabins to hide themselves.

The army advanced, firing volley after volley till they came up to the cabins. They set every one of them on fire and all that were in them, men, women and children, innocent and guilty, even all burned together in one common mass.

I knew one man myself as peaceable and inoffensive a man as any in town, who ran out of his bed in his shirt and an infant in his arms and was shot dead at his own door—for the orders given out were to spare no man that was not in regimentals.

At Tara Hill, County Meath, several thousand rebels had gathered to threaten the capital and cut communications to the north. Several hundred Highland Fencibles and local Yeomanry attacked and did terrible execution with an artillery bombardment. Some 350 bodies were discovered on the battlefield; the casualty figures for the government forces were a mere thirteen dead and twenty-eight wounded. At Rathangan, where the rebels had occupied the town, they were dislodged by cannon.

It was a similar story at Ballitore, home village of the Quaker diarist Mary Leadbeater. She soon had more horrors to confide to her journal, for the occupying soldiers shot, hanged and looted with little discrimination.

This party of soldiers entered Ballitore exhausted by rage and fatigue. They brought cannon. The trumpet was sounded and the peaceable inhabitants were delivered up for two hours to the unbridled licence of a furious soldiery.

My mind never could arrange the transactions which were crowded into those two hours. Every house in the Burrow was in flames. We saw soldiers bending under loads of plunder. Some of their countenances were pale with anger, and they grinned at me, calling me names I had never heard before.

I beheld from the back window of our parlour the dark red flames of Ganin's house and others rising above the green of the trees. A fat tobacconist from the town lolled upon one of our chairs and boasted of the exploits of the military whom he had accompanied, how they had shot several rebels, adding: 'We burned one fellow in a tar barrel.' I never in my life felt disgust so strongly …

At Rathangan, where the rebels had murdered some loyalist prisoners (and allegedly nailed the head of a Yeoman officer, Thomas Spenser, to his own front door), the army exacted a similarly savage retribution.

This illustration, dating from the 1898 centenary commemoration, recalls that the seizing of mail coaches was the signal for the outbreak of the rising.

After the shock of insurrection, these victories for the armed forces of the Crown were cheering for loyalists; nonetheless the number of the rebels, their determination and their ferocity enjoined prudence on the officers in command. After his success at Kilcullen, General Dundas, perhaps mindful of the initial fate of his cavalry against pikemen well dug in at Old Kilcullen churchyard, had been unwilling to venture further, and, to loyalist fury, he had retired to Naas. Moreover, convinced that the rebels now recognised the folly of their actions, he began to discuss terms of surrender with those camped at Knockallen Hill and at Gibbet Rath on the Curragh plain.

The seemingly humane—and apparently genuine—amnesty was the prelude to wholesale slaughter. Dublin Castle wholly disapproved of any terms other than unconditional surrender, but Dundas had gone ahead anyway and settled with the rebels at Knockallen on 28 May.

It was to be a different story at the Curragh a day later. There, proceedings to accept the surrender of several thousand rebels were nearing completion when Sir James Duff's men—largely Dublin Militia—arrived on the scene, having marched from Limerick to reopen the road to Dublin. The Militia were in no mood for amnesties. The commanding officer's seventeen-year-old son, Lieutenant William Giffard, had been shot and piked when seized by rebels on the mail coach in Kildare. Already inflamed at the discovery of the corpse, the soldiers were in a vengeful mood when they came across the surrender. Duff reported what happened next.

> I sent on some of the Yeomen to tell them [the rebels] that on laying down their arms, they should not be hurt. Unfortunately some of them fired on the troops: from that moment they were attacked on all sides: nothing could stop the rage of the troops. I believe two to three hundred rebels were killed. We have three men killed and several wounded. I am too much fatigued to enlarge.

Whether or not the surrendering rebels fired first on Duff's men will never be known; what is certain is that hundreds of unarmed men were mercilessly shot and sabred, and that Duff was acclaimed a hero on his arrival at Dublin. Captain John Giffard exulted.

Edward Hepenstall, the walking gallows: this image dates from 1810 and is unlikely to be a true image of Hepenstall.

'My troops did not leave my hero [his son William] unavenged—500 rebels bleaching on the Curragh of Kildare—that Curragh over which my sweet innocent girls walked with me last summer, that Curragh was strewed with the vile carcasses of popish rebels and the accursed town of Kildare has been reduced to a heap of ashes by our hands.'

As for Dundas, he found himself denounced: so far from allowing clemency to the rebels, wrote one commentator, 'it was the general opinion here they should all have been put to death.'

By the end of the first four days' fighting the rebels had been routed in and around Dublin, though not in County Wicklow. Moreover, the capital had been secured. Suspects were flogged at the rear of Dublin Castle. In the barracks off St Stephen's Green Lieutenant Edward Hepenstall of the Wicklow Militia became known as the Walking Gallows from his practice of garrotting rebel suspects—suspected, that is, by him—with his own neckerchief while they hung over his back. Sometimes he jogged to assist the process; according to the horrified loyalist Sir Jonah Barrington, crowds gathered to laugh and applaud.

Other rebel dead were exposed to view in the Castle courtyard or draped from bridges over the Liffey. House-burning in the Liberties had the effect of driving aspirant insurgents away to join their comrades outside the city. So the threat of insurgency in the city had receded. Communications north and south had been reopened.

And yet the Castle could not rest easy. The resolution of the rebels, their apparent indifference to casualties and, again, their sheer numbers all acted powerfully against official complacency. In addition, the loyalists' clamour for blood, their portrayal of the rebellion as a Popish plot or a re-enactment of 1641 was deeply worrying for the Castle. Not for the first time the hapless Lord Lieutenant,

Limberlip, the priest killer, shooting at a priest. The rebellion had inevitable sectarian overtones, despite the secular idealism of the United Irish leaders.

Camden, wrung his hands and declared that 'the feelings of [the loyalists] … are so exasperated as scarcely to be satisfied with anything short of extirpation.'

From the beginning, the rebellion had taken on a sectarian cast. Such a development may have been inevitable, given the balance of power within the Protestant Irish state, given that state's interpretation of the entire United Irish project, and given its determination to fly its flag above the stronghold of Protestant Ascendancy. No doubt also the Orange hue of the military excesses during the 'pre-rebellion' was hugely conducive to this development.

The rebels also made their contribution. The insurgents at Dunboyne, County Meath, had succumbed to their desire for revenge and had subscribed to the agenda drawn up by the confessional state. 'The rebels took seven prisoners,' it was reported, 'four of them Protestant were massacred, the three Papists were let go.' At Rathangan some nineteen Protestants were led out and massacred, while Catholic loyalists were spared. Giffard's son may have been killed by the Kildare rebels because he was an army officer; but to his loving father he was murdered because he was a Protestant. The 1641 comet was again visible.

The bridge across the Slaney at Enniscorthy, in the centre of Co. Wexford, with the castle in the background

Wexford

> Yesterday, advices were received from Lieutenant Colonel Foote, of the North Cork Regiment of Militia, that having advanced with one hundred men against a very numerous body of rebels, his party was attacked when exhausted by the length of their march and, after killing a great number of the enemy, it was almost entirely cut off.

This terse communiqué from Dublin Castle, dated Tuesday 29 May 1798, confirmed the rumours that had swept Dublin a day earlier. For the first time in the rebellion a detachment of troops, in this case over a hundred men of the North Cork Militia, at Oulart, County Wexford, had been cut to pieces in an open engagement. Only Colonel Foote, a veteran of the American war, a sergeant and two privates survived to tell the tale. The pattern evident in Counties Dublin, Kildare and Meath, of violent outbreaks followed by rebel defeats and massacres, had changed. Wexford was ablaze.

For Dublin Castle, the eruption of County Wexford was a most unexpected as well as a most unwelcome development. In the months and years before the rebellion Wexford had, by and large, escaped official scrutiny. The Castle had had very few informants or informers in that county and, most unwisely, had clearly considered this lack of information as pointing towards a general quiescence among the people.

More immediate reassurance concerning County Wexford came from the complete absence of returns of United Irishmen in that county among the lists seized at Oliver Bond's house in the swoop of March 1798. (The Castle did not know that this was because the Wexford delegate was apparently delayed while drinking in the Bleeding Horse tavern en route to the meeting and had arrived after the arrests at Bond's had taken place.) Then again, in mid-May 1798 the authorities had been persuaded by the 'loyalty' campaign of the local political magnate, Lord Mountnorris, by which, through the agency of priests, large quantities of arms had been surrendered by the disaffected in the county. All in all, in the eyes of Dublin Castle, County Wexford was an unlikely and an unexpected setting for determined insurrection.

And yet close observers—and some not so close—were not taken in by the apparent tranquillity. County Wexford had long been divided along religious lines, for seventeenth-century settlement patterns had exercised a persistent influence on its political and religious geography. Significantly, the county had the largest Protestant settlement outside Ulster. Its politics had long been poisoned by sectarianism, for the Protestant governing elite in the county had split into an 'Ascendancy' faction, headed by the likes of George Ogle and Hunter Gowan, and a liberal wing, centred around Beauchamp Bagenal Harvey and the Colclough family of Tintern.

John Henry Colclough of Tintern

A large number of interlocking wealthy Catholic families, boasting priests, strong farmers and middlemen among their members and connected politically with the liberal Protestants, were also a powerful presence in the county. In recent times an economic recession had resulted from the collapse of the malt and barley trade between Wexford and Dublin; this had sharpened resentments, which, because of the structure of county politics, had inevitably been cast in a sectarian mould.

All this was well known. Sir Jonah Barrington, visiting County Wexford socially in the weeks before the rebellion, had noted the rebellious and republican sentiments of even sound Protestant gentlemen like Bagenal Harvey. In June 1798 the politically astute Lady Louisa Conolly observed from her vantage point in Kildare: 'At Wexford there has so far back as 36 years to my knowledge existed a violent Protestant and Catholic party. Consequently those engines were set to work for the purpose of rebellion.'

Two developments pitched County Wexford over the edge and into full-scale rebellion. The first was the campaign of terror unleashed, particularly in the north of the county, from mid-May 1798 onwards. The second was the very fact of a crushing rebel victory at Oulart.

The terror was unrelenting. From 20 May half-hangings, floggings, pitch-cappings and house-burnings, conducted principally by the North Cork Militia under the direction of magistrates such as Hawtrey White, Hunter Gowan and Archibald Jacob, inflamed that part of the county that bordered on County Wicklow and induced panic everywhere. There was a constant fear that 'the Orangemen' planned a general massacre, and people took to sleeping out of their houses at night lest they be slaughtered in their beds.

After 23 May the campaign against the United men reached new levels of ferocity. The torture by pitch-capping of Anthony Perry of Inch, a Protestant leader of the United Irishmen, led him to divulge the names of others, and they in their turn were hunted down and, if caught, similarly treated. As the 'croppy-hunt' spread south from north County Wexford, near-hysteria gripped the county as a whole. Hunter Gowan's triumphant entry into Gorey, riding a horse and holding aloft his sword with the severed finger of one of his victims on it, was hardly calculated to reassure.

Then on 26 May came stunning news. At Dunlavin in south County Wicklow some thirty-four suspected United men had been summarily put to death by the garrison; and at Carnew, across the border in County Wexford, thirty-five prisoners had been taken out and shot in a ball-alley. Fevered rumours of massacre now appeared to have substance. In terror, the peasantry—United Irishmen or not—prepared to resist.

The second catalyst was the rebel victory at Oulart Hill. After a minor skirmish at the Harrow, in which a prominent magistrate, Bookey, and two Yeomen were killed, about a thousand rebels, led by their local priest, Father John Murphy, gathered on Oulart Hill, to the east of Enniscorthy. It was there, on 27 May, that a detachment of the North Cork Militia rashly attacked them and was cut to pieces. The soldiers had been enticed into an ambush near the summit, then raked with musket fire and pursued ruthlessly with pikes. The Corkmen, many of them Catholics, appealed to their fellow-Irishmen for mercy. Some reportedly spoke Irish; others brandished scapulars, signs of their Catholic faith. This Militia unit was the same one that had gained a name for pitch-capping rebel suspects in the midlands during the preceding weeks. At Oulart, they were shown no mercy.

An 1898 centenary illustration of the Battle of Oulart Hill

This victory in an open engagement, the first for the rebels anywhere, electrified the county, tempting many to join in who might otherwise have hung back. Undoubtedly it re-ignited a rebellion in Leinster that earlier had shown every sign of petering out. Further afield, news of the rebels' success at Oulart sparked renewed efforts to raise the hitherto quiescent Counties Antrim and Down.

On 28 May, Father Murphy rested and considered what to do next. His decision was that he would maintain the rebel initiative and attack Enniscorthy. On 29 May the insurgents, gaining strength as they advanced, stormed the town. It was defended by several hundred Yeomen and Militia, but they were overwhelmed by the thousands of rebel pikemen and marksmen. The defences were swept aside by means of a cattle stampede, and behind the terrified animals came the rebels. No quarter was given: anyone thought to look like an Orangeman was piked on the spot. The town was set on fire; the pall of smoke rising above it could be seen nearly twenty miles away.

Father John Murphy of Boolavogue

The aftermath was one of desolation. Pigs and dogs gorged on the roasted and half-roasted bodies of those piked and burnt. Local and sectarian enmities broke out under the guise of war as victors took revenge on vanquished loyalists.

In Dublin Castle the response was one of shock. The Chief Secretary, Castlereagh, wrote of his apprehensions regarding the Wexford phenomenon:

> The Rebellion in Wexford has assumed a more serious shape than was to be apprehended from a peasantry, however well organised.
>
> The enemy are in great force. Their numbers consist of the entire male inhabitants of Wexford and the greatest proportion of those of Wicklow, Kildare, Carlow and Kilkenny. From Carlow to Dublin, I am told, scarcely an inhabitant is to be seen.
>
> The face of the country [is] so broken and enclosed that regular formations are impracticable ... so as to make it prudent to assemble a very considerable force

before any attempt is made to penetrate that very difficult country ...

Rely upon it there never was in any country so formidable an effort on the part of the people. Our force cannot cope in a variety of distant points with an enemy that can elude attack where it is inexpedient to risk a contest.

The government hold on County Wexford had slipped. Gorey in turn was quickly abandoned by the forces of the Crown, the local Yeomanry thoughtfully shooting their prisoners in the street before fleeing. And the next day the rebels, by now possibly fifteen thousand strong, turned their attention to the town of Wexford.

Duncannon Fort on the Barrow estuary

The county capital was in fact quite defensible. It was garrisoned by several hundred Yeomen and Militiamen, and its defences were in the capable hands of Lieutenant-Colonel Jonas Watson, a retired regular officer. He enthusiastically built barricades and stripped the houses of combustible material: Wexford was not to burn like Enniscorthy. Moreover, reinforcements, including much-needed artillery and gunners, were on their way from Duncannon to the west.

Then disaster struck. The relief forces, about a hundred strong, were spotted by insurgent look-outs some miles from Wexford, and an attack, led by Thomas Cloney, was launched on them. The rebels achieved complete surprise, and at close quarters their pikes were truly formidable. As happened at Oulart, within minutes the enemy was almost entirely wiped out: about a dozen soldiers were made prisoner; a few dazed survivors made their way back to Taghmon with the grim news. It was another stunning victory. Moreover, the rebels now had cannon with which to shell Wexford. General Fawcett ruefully drew the lesson of his men's impetuosity:

A view of Wexford town from the northern side of the bridge

Any attempt that was not next to a certainty of succeeding against the rebels should never again be attempted. Believe me, they are no longer to be despised as common armed peasantry. They are organised and have persons of skill and enterprise among them.

The diary of Elizabeth Richards of Rathaspick House, just outside Wexford, captures the apprehension of the peaceable loyalist population as the rebels—many of them recognised as neighbours, both Catholic and Protestant—took over civil society.

> During the night the rebels had collected in great force at the Three Rocks. Through the telescope we plainly saw them in large bodies marching and counter-marching and holding their pikes as in joy.
>
> In the morning a man rode into the courtyard with a green bow in his hat and a drawn sword. The servants seemed joyful. 'We are starving, m'am,' said he to Mrs. Hatton. 'Send us provisions or —' And he struck his sword with violence on the head of a pump and rode off. His orders were instantly complied with.

Miles Byrne in old age

Wexford's fate was sealed when Colonel Watson ventured outside the town to survey the rebel position. He was shot dead by a single shot from a marksman firing the local long-barrelled fowling-musket. Seconds later a shell from a rebel howitzer, just captured from Fawcett's men, burst in front of Watson's escort of soldiers. All thoughts of defence were now given up, and Wexford was abandoned.

The elated rebels speedily took possession of the town; but in the euphoria of victory they could not be persuaded to pursue the retreating soldiers. When the celebrations had died down it was discovered that almost all the military stores had been taken by those in retreat. It was also discovered that a number of Yeomen had sought to conceal themselves in houses in the town, and some had attempted to flee by ship. Those found were roughly dragged out and installed in the town jail, which was soon crammed to the door.

The fall of Wexford was the high point of the rebellion in the county, but with the benefit of hindsight it could be argued that this signal triumph for the rebels in the end turned out to be rather a hollow victory. Certainly, in years to come Miles Byrne, a rebel captain and later a *chef de bataillon* (major) in Bonaparte's army, would bitterly lament

Father Murphy's decision to make for Wexford rather than New Ross after the fall of Enniscorthy. The decision, he argued, gave the Crown forces a vital few days during which to fortify this gateway to the south. Success at Wexford was excellent for morale, and it certainly sent shock waves through Dublin Castle, but it had the effect of corralling the rebellion within the confines of County Wexford. Would the rebels be able to break out?

The Wexford Republic

After the fall of Wexford the United Irish leaders in the county had reasserted their authority. In the newly formed 'Wexford Republic' a Committee of Public Safety was set up, under Captain Mathew Keogh, a retired British army officer. Its membership was to be equally balanced between Catholics and Protestants; its purpose was to regulate food supplies, prevent looting, and maintain order in the town. Certainly among loyalist citizens there was near-panic. Elizabeth Richards of Rathaspick House recorded in her diary:

> About 6 o'clock vast numbers of the insurgents on horse back and on foot marched from the Three Rocks to take possession of the town.
>
> In the town there were distressing scenes. The shops all shut, pike men guarding every avenue. Houses gutted, the streets strewn with broken glass, furniture, articles of ladies' dresses. Confusion, astonishment, exaltation, ferocity were alternately reflected in the faces of those we met.
>
> A boy of about 14, a relation of Bagenal Harvey, made something in the street. The mob collected around him asking if they should not get a pitch cap for Lord Kingsborough. The mob wanted to see him and have him taken.
>
> Several Protestants, terrified at a report that a massacre was intended, had abjured their faith and suffered themselves to be christened by Romanish priests from whom they had obtained written protections.

In a further attempt at cooling the sectarian temper, the Protestant landlord and long-time United Irishman Bagenal Harvey was made commander-in-chief. Father John Murphy of Boolavogue, despite his exploits at Oulart and Enniscorthy, was not considered for the overall rebel command. In the event, Harvey proved an uninspired choice: in his *Memoirs*, Miles Byrne later claimed that Harvey had been chosen in order to give the lie to the claim that the rebellion was purely a Catholic movement.

Despite these efforts to put a non-sectarian face on the rebellion, there were from an early day worrying signs of religious rancour. Understandably, in view of the earlier massacres of Catholics, there were demands that loyalists be punished, but these were successfully resisted. However, Protestant prisoners were forced to form a firing party to execute a Catholic informer, and there were reports of Protestants being urged to renounce their religion and declare themselves to be Catholic. For the time being, confessional fury was held in check; but it was anyone's guess what would happen should rebel discipline collapse.

Campaigns in Wexford, 30 May to 9 June

On 31 May the Wexford army divided into three. A northern division was directed to launch an attack on Gorey, which had been reoccupied by the army, and then to push on into County Wicklow; another column was deputed to capture Newtownbarry (Bunclody); and a southern division, under Bagenal Harvey himself, would meanwhile take New Ross. In this way—it was intended—the rebellion would be spread into Counties Waterford and Kilkenny.

Things went badly from the start. In north Wexford the rebels were beaten back at Newtownbarry, suffering some five hundred casualties. Inexperience told against them: they had in fact captured the town but a swift counter-attack by the King's County Militia caused them to flee. A few miles away a rebel column on its way to seize Gorey was surprised and scattered, with over a hundred casualties. At both Newtownbarry and Gorey government losses were negligible, and, eager to bring rebellion to a conclusion before the French arrived (or Ulster rose), armies under General Loftus at Gorey and Lord Ancram at Newtownbarry prepared to move south.

Their advance, however, was checked at Tubberneering in north County Wexford when on 5 June the inexperienced and impetuous Colonel Walpole, keen to prove himself in battle, hurled his men at the rebels. His column of five hundred men was ambushed; Walpole fell in the first volley of musket fire, and after a desperate battle his men were scattered, with great losses. Several pieces of artillery were captured by the rebels, as well as badly needed military stores. The initiative in north Wexford once again passed to the rebels.

The day after the victory at Tubberneering the southern division of the Wexford army hurled itself at New Ross, the strategically vital town on the Wexford-Kilkenny border. It was a crucial point. The town's fall would have ignited the entire south-central area of Ireland and would certainly have opened the way for the rebels to move into County Waterford and to threaten Cork. Now the decision to take Wexford began to tell. Major-General Henry Johnston, in command at New Ross, had been given precious days to attend to the town's defences, and he had spent his time profitably. Trenches were dug at the main entry points, and Johnston had positioned his men in strongholds within the town as well.

Major-General Henry Johnston, commander of Crown forces at New Ross

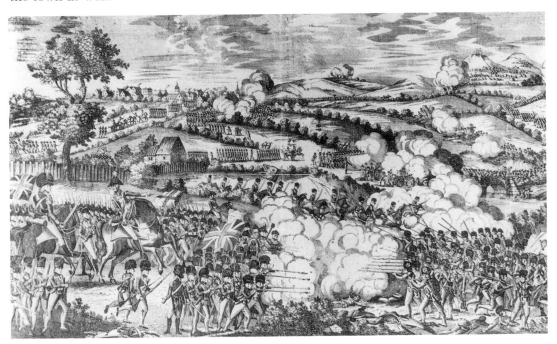

A general view of the Battle of New Ross

For a time the result of the battle hung in the balance. The rebels, estimated at ten thousand strong, had attacked at dawn, 'shouting and driving cattle before them' and forcing the defenders to fall back before the enormous press of pikemen. During the battle the attackers had displayed reckless courage, while sustaining horrendous casualties. 'I never saw any troops attack with more enthusiasm and bravery than the rebels did on the 5th,' wrote Lieutenant-Colonel Robert Craufurd, later to distinguish himself in the Peninsular War. The defence of the town had been entrusted to detachments of the Dublin, Donegal, Clare and Meath Militia, the Midlothian Fencibles, and units of artillery and cavalry, mostly the 5th Dragoons. In the face of the overwhelming rebel numbers, the government soldiers also fought bravely.

Cruikshank's cartoon of a rebel stuffing his wig in the cannon's mouth in the belief that it had stopped. It had not: a moment later it fired.

The battle raged for hours. At one point the government troops retreated across the bridge to the Waterford side. The rebels failed to capitalise. A counter-attack, and

119

sustained cannon and musket fire, began to tell. The rebels were exhausted and confused and their arms insufficient (one loyalist eye-witness reported how the rebel musket balls fell short, indicating poor powder). In the end, artillery decided the battle, and the rebels retreated. Official returns listed ninety soldiers killed and fifty-seven wounded. Rebel casualties were shattering: their army was now only about two thousand strong and their wounded and captured—and indeed many local non-combatants—fell victim to an indiscriminate military retribution. Many wounded were reportedly burnt alive in the town buildings. One loyalist, James Alexander, described the scene:

> I saw the streets literally strewed with dead carcasses. The greatest slaughter was in the Main Street. 'Twas horrible. Many were reduced to ashes, many carcasses to a cinder. On the belly of a half-roasted rebel lay a Roman Catholic prayer-book open at the Office for the Dead.

The Battle of New Ross

Those who survived may have been in shock; for many the realisation must have dawned that victory was impossible, and that even surrender might not be accepted. Tensions were high; and the day's slaughter had not yet ended.

As the rebels had begun to retreat from New Ross they had come across their comrades who had been left behind a few miles away at Scullabogue to guard more than a hundred loyalist prisoners—men, women, and children. These apparent hostages were almost entirely Protestant, but there were a few Catholics among them. Their guards were repeatedly urged by fleeing rebels to kill them, and though they resisted for a time they gave in by late morning. Some twenty men were led out and shot, while the remainder, mostly women and children, were locked in a barn, which was then fired. Within minutes the barn was an inferno; there were no survivors. It was an atrocity to set beside those perpetrated by government forces; ever since it has been profoundly symbolic of the entire rebellion in Leinster.

Cruikshank's famous drawing of the massacre at Scullabogue, perhaps the most potent propaganda image of the entire rebellion

Henry Joy McCracken

Rebuffed in the south-west of County Wexford, the rebels turned their attention once more to the north. An advance was made on the strategically sited town of Arklow at a river crossing in coastal south Wicklow. Once again the rebels appeared to acquit themselves well: in Miles Byrne's opinion, 'our very irregular troops against a regular and disciplined English army' might have carried the day, but for some confusion over orders. In the event, after much slaughter—perhaps three hundred rebel dead—they were repulsed by soldiers under General Francis Needham and, without clear objectives, fell back to regroup at the vantage point of Vinegar Hill, outside Enniscorthy. For the moment, that camp remained intact. The government was loath to move in force against the rebels until the promised reinforcements had arrived from England. In the meantime, Dublin Castle was content that the rebellion had been sealed in to Wexford and that the rebels could not now break out in force.

But Wexford was no longer the government's only problem.

Ulster rises, 7–13 June

While rebellion had been raging in the south-east, the north generally had been quiet. On 29 May, on receiving news of the fighting in Leinster, the Ulster Provincial Council of the United Irishmen had held a stormy meeting. Loud protests were raised at the failure to rise in support. The existing leadership was accused (by Henry Joy McCracken and John Hughes, both of Belfast) of having 'completely betrayed the people both of Leinster and Ulster' and was promptly deposed.

In fact McCracken's strictures were largely misplaced. The plan for insurrection had called for the

Lord O'Neill of Shane's Castle, who died at the Battle of Antrim

risen Dublin to be sealed off by risings in the surrounding counties; the city would be secured and reinforcements prevented from reaching it. It was the failure of this strategy that now fuelled demands for a rising in the north. As in County Wexford, what had been intended as a diversion or side show to the main event in the Dublin area was now thrust into prominence.

The Battle of Antrim

Following McCracken's outburst, the military command of the United Irishmen in Ulster was reorganised, and plans were hurriedly made for a rising. Out of twenty-three United Irish colonels in County Antrim, only two had declared for action; 'the other twenty-one would not act on any plan but on the invasion of the French or success to the efforts of the insurgents about Dublin.'

New men, McCracken among them, were now appointed. Word of these stirrings reached Dublin Castle. 'I hear there is a buzz in parts of the north which I like not,' wrote Edward Cooke on 31 May. But it was not until 7 June that General Nugent received word that an attack on Antrim was likely: the object of the rebels, it quickly appeared, was to seize the magistrates assembling in the town. He moved swiftly; there were some arrests, and the magistrates were prevented from walking into a trap. 'We have brought in many prisoners,' wrote an officer from the camp at Blaris, 'and we are taking more today, hanging some etc.'

Despite these precautions, a large number of rebels assembled in different parts of County Antrim on 7 June. In Ballymena the Green Flag was raised over the market house, and there were attacks on Larne, Glenarm, Carrickfergus, and Ballymoney. At Toomebridge, where the River Bann flows out of Lough Neagh, the rebels secured the main route north-west from Belfast. From their camp at Donegore Hill, the rebels set out for the town of Antrim.

Once again it was a story of early success, then rapid failure. Moving down the main street of Antrim from All Saints' Church, the rebels wrought havoc on infantry and cavalry, cutting reins and riders with their pikes. Lord O'Neill of Antrim Castle was fatally wounded and his forces briefly driven back behind the castle walls. But in the rapidity of their movement on the day, the rebels had failed to post guards on the roads. Reinforcements poured in, and the tide was turned. McCracken's forces were then driven out, 'with great slaughter,' by artillery fire.

Colonel Durham, who commanded the attacking force, reckoned that 150 rebels had died in the streets; and, as happened elsewhere, the army could not be stopped from burning the town. 'Although the insurrection has been pretty general in the county,' noted General Nugent with immense self-satisfaction, 'I do not find they had much success.' An attempted mobilisation in County Derry came to nothing, and by the evening of 8 June the Antrim rebels had lost heart and had begun drifting home. Nugent's proclamation offering leniency to all but 'leaders' may have helped make up a few minds that the situation was hopeless. Ballymena,

Major-General George Nugent

Randalstown and Toomebridge were quickly recaptured.

As the rising elsewhere in the north was petering out, the United Irishmen in County Down began to assemble their forces, at Scrabo Hill outside Newtownards, then at Saintfield. On 9 June they took both Saintfield and Newtownards, though an attack on Portaferry failed. The next day—known thereafter as 'Pike Sunday'—Colonel Stapleton, exhibiting a similar rashness to that which had cost Walpole his life at Tubberneering, advanced with his men from Comber to attack the rebels at Saintfield, without waiting for either orders or reinforcements.

The Battle of Ballynahinch

Stapleton was ambushed outside Saintfield and, ignominiously, was pinned down on the ground for hours by rebel marksmen. Nugent would not venture to relieve him, in case Belfast rose, and it was the following day before reinforcements arrived, enabling Stapleton to make his retreat to Comber. Unlike Walpole, Stapleton survived, but his men and officers had sustained 'very severe' casualties. An early estimate reckoned over fifty army dead.

Having received intelligence that Belfast was secure, Nugent marched his main force towards the rebels at Saintfield, while another force advanced against the rebels from Downpatrick to the south. Nugent's war train was reported to be over two miles long: from south Down the rebels could see it approach.

The rebels were led by Henry Munro, a shopkeeper from Newtownards, and a

Defender named Magennis, who had brought Catholic fighters to join the Presbyterians. The rebels moved their camp from Saintfield to Ballynahinch, a few miles down the road, and camped on Ednavady Hill above the town, while the troops roamed the streets below. That night Munro reportedly refused, out of a sense of honour, to attack the government troops under cover of darkness as they lay drunk and sleeping in Ballynahinch below. Hundreds of his men deserted in disgust or fear as the chance was forgone.

When battle was joined on 12–13 June at Ballynahinch the rebels were routed by Nugent. Several hundred were killed, many of them as they sought to hide in the woods of Lord Moira's estate nearby. Munro was taken and, a few days later, hanged outside his front door. Nugent lost only three men and listed some thirty wounded. Saintfield and Ballynahinch were both burnt to the ground.

A nineteenth-century painting by John Carey depicting the hanging of Henry Joy McCracken

Much grim amusement was derived from Lord Moira's discomfiture at the number of rebel dead in his pleasure park, for he had been the principal critic of Dublin Castle's counter-insurgency policy. With heavy sarcasm, Cooke reported that 'the countenances of his Lordship's tenants were beaming with loyalty' on the arrival of General Nugent before Moira's gutted mansion.

In the end, very few of the United Irishmen in either Antrim or Down had really been prepared for combat in 1798—principally, it would seem, because the United Irish military plan had centred on Dublin. In addition, government action in 1796–97 had undoubtedly disrupted their organisation severely. It is possible also that the worsening image of revolutionary, martial France had caused a loss of enthusiasm for either a French landing or French principles. Those who did turn out rarely displayed any significant military talent, indeed scarcely appeared to know what to do.

One rebel commander of the 'Republican Army of the County Down', from his later exile in the United States, described his campaign in and around north Down thus: 'Instead of the [rebel] forces meeting at any point in collected and organised bodies, they met rather more by accident than design and they were in no better order than a country mob ... when thus assembled, without provisions, without officers and without any military subordination.'

It is possible that, as Cooke put it, 'the Popish tinge in the Rebellion' had induced second thoughts among the Presbyterian rebels, causing them to hang back; and General Knox, usually a shrewd observer, told him to 'depend upon it, the Presbyterians will not abet a Catholic plot.' Certainly, on the night before the Battle of Ballynahinch there was a revealing incident when the rebel commanders, Munro and Magennis, disputed the overall command. Munro finally drew his sword and allegedly 'did declare aloud his intention was to establish a presbiterian independent government after the begun revolution would become compleated.' Magennis was understandably unimpressed with this objective, and he and his men reportedly stole away during the night.

Vinegar Hill, 21 June

With the rebels scattered in the north, attention shifted once again to those in County Wexford. Government plans were now laid to attack their camp at Vinegar Hill. Reinforcements from England had by this time begun arriving (nine thousand infantry and cavalry by mid-June). These facilitated General Lake's plan to assemble the army that would finally crush the rebellion in County Wexford and, as the Chief Secretary, Castlereagh, had urged, 'make the rebels there an example to the rest of the kingdom.' Lake was no Bonaparte, but then he didn't need to be, for the rebels had played into his hands by their decision to encamp on Vinegar Hill. Years later, Miles Byrne pondered the question: 'How could our leaders for an instant think that Vinegar Hill was a military position susceptible of defence for any time without provisions, military stores or great guns?'

The rebel camp on Vinegar Hill

By 20 June, Lake had assembled an army of some twenty thousand men and a vast array of artillery before the rebel encampment. The pikemen were stretched out along the ridge running east from the hilltop away from Enniscorthy. Lake's preparations had not been easy: his subordinate commanders had frequent cause for complaint about his

Two views of the Battle of Vinegar Hill

'extraordinary and contradictory orders,' and the indiscipline of the soldiers also hampered his plans. General Francis Needham, fresh from his triumph at Arklow, reported that his troops were too exhausted to go to Vinegar Hill, for they had wasted their energies in killing 'above 100 fugitives on their way here [about six miles from Vinegar Hill] this day whom they found conceal'd in ditches.' Ironically, it was Needham's failure to close the ring around Vinegar Hill that was to allow the rebels to retreat in tolerable order after the battle.

On 21 June, Lake attempted to surround Vinegar Hill with four columns of soldiers, in order to prevent a rebel break-out. Battle was then joined. It lasted about two hours. The rebels, as Miles Byrne was to lament afterwards, had made little effort to dig in or to erect defences against artillery or infantry; they appeared to expect to draw troops towards them for close combat. Instead they were mercilessly shelled while the government infantry advanced with little challenge.

The thump of the cannons could be heard, at dawn, almost twenty miles south in Wexford. Once again artillery carried the day. The insurgent army was not massacred: as Needham failed to close the offensive loop, they fought until their ammunition ran out, and then many—perhaps most—fled south from the hill and escaped towards County Wicklow or to the west towards County Kilkenny. 'The rascals made a tolerable good fight of it,' wrote Lake, adding, 'the carnage was dreadful'; though the men escaped in great numbers, hundreds of camp-followers, principally women, died on the field of battle.

In his despatch announcing his victory, Lake singled out the commander of the Midlothian Fencibles, Lord Ancram, for special praise for his conduct during the battle, and the Midlothians soon found themselves singing a new regimental song.

> Ye croppies of Wexford, I'd have ye be wise
> And go not to meddle with Midlothian Boys,
> For the Midlothian Boys they vow and declare

They'll crop off your head as well as your hair.
  Derry-down, down.
Remember at Ross and at Vinegar Hill
How your heads flew about like chaff in a mill,
For the Midlothian Boys when a croppy they see
They blow out his daylights and tip him cut three.
  Derry-down, down.

It was the last formal battle. The momentum was now firmly with the government, and the rebels' objective was to survive, cross country, and regroup. Heavy casualties were sustained as the rebels attempted to break out of County Wexford. General Asgill reported two hundred dead at Goresbridge on the Barrow, and Lord Clifden, with his Yeomanry, reported an implausible thousand dead at Leighlinbridge.

The executions on Wexford bridge

Castlecomer was burnt by the rebels as they fell back; and there were occasional ferocious skirmishes elsewhere, notably at Baltinglass (thirty carloads of rebel dead carried away), Kilconnell Hill in County Wicklow (where now General Asgill claimed a thousand rebels killed), and at Kilbeggan, County Westmeath (thirty to forty rebel casualties). The defeated rebels also showed that they still had the capacity to sting—and more: on 30 June, at Ballyellis in north County Wexford, a large cavalry detachment was cut to pieces in an ambush. The rebel leader, the very able 'General' Joseph Holt, may have overstated the casualties if not the violence of the engagement:

> In less than 20 minutes there were 370 of the King's troops slain. Our loss was but four wounded. A black trumpeter was most tenacious of life, he took more piking than five white men. Before he expired, a fellow cut off his ears for the sake of the gold rings and put them in his pocket. The trumpeter, during his torture, exclaimed passwords of a United Irishman.

And in County Wicklow, Holt and another insurgent leader, Michael Dwyer, proved a constant thorn in the side of the government for a long time.

The capture of Bagenal Harvey on the Saltee Islands

Edward Cooke in Dublin Castle was exasperated at the rebels' refusal to surrender quietly. 'I could not suppose such obduracy,' he exclaimed. 'The mere [i.e. true] republicans submitted at once in the north. The papist fanatic is hardly to be subdued at all.' The government personnel was changing. Camden departed. The new Lord Lieutenant, Marquis Cornwallis, took a much more relaxed view: on 8 July he wrote that while there were certainly small groups of rebels in Counties Wicklow, Wexford, Kildare, Meath and Dublin there was now no actual force in arms. After Vinegar Hill, the rebellion in the south-east was, in effect, over.

Aftermath

In defeat, rebel discipline had collapsed in some places. The reverse at New Ross had led to the mass killing of more than a hundred loyalists at Scullabogue; and now, following the disaster at Vinegar Hill, about seventy Protestant prisoners were piked to death on the bridge in Wexford. The army repaid these atrocities with interest: the mopping-up operations after Vinegar Hill resembled, to the fury of Lord Cornwallis, little more than universal rape, plunder, and murder. 'Any man in a brown coat who is found within several miles of the seat of action is butchered without discrimination,' he protested; and even General Lake, by no means faint-hearted, complained that his men's 'determination to destroy everyone they think is a rebel is beyond description and wants much correction.'

This lust for rebel blood was fuelled at the highest level in Dublin Castle. 'The conversation even at my table', reported Cornwallis in dismay, 'always turns on hanging, shooting, burning etc. etc. and if a priest has been put to death, the greatest joy is expressed by the whole company.' In Wexford itself some thirty Catholic chapels were burnt, presumably at the hands of the local Yeomanry, in the months after the rebellion; and something approaching a 'White terror' was installed everywhere as, on all sides, loyalists demanded vengeance.

Retribution was at first swift and generally uncompromising. Bagenal Harvey, the Protestant commander in Wexford, was captured on the Saltee Islands, swiftly tried, and hanged; and so too were the prominent rebel leaders Cornelius Grogan, Mathew Keogh, and Anthony Perry (all Protestants). Their heads were cut off and stuck on spikes outside the courthouse in Wexford. Father John Murphy, the hero of Oulart and Enniscorthy (or a latter-day mixture of Attila, Genghis Khan and Tamerlane, as loyalists saw him), was captured in Tullow, County Carlow. He was stripped, mercilessly flogged, hanged and decapitated and his corpse burnt in a barrel. With an eye for detail, the local Yeomanry spiked his head on a building directly opposite the local Catholic church and, with great glee, forced the Catholics of Tullow to open their windows to admit the 'holy smoke' from Murphy's funeral pyre.

The French in Killala Bay *by William Sadler*

Such vengefulness, however, affronted the Lord Lieutenant, and he moved swiftly to put a halt to it. From his arrival in Ireland in mid-June, Cornwallis made determined efforts to end the undisciplined military repression with which large areas of the country were threatened. The entire country was still under martial law, and courts-martial—at that time little more than hastily assembled tribunals consisting of a few junior officers— were everywhere dispensing capital sentences, transportations and floggings as they saw fit.

Cornwallis immediately demanded that all sentences handed down be referred to him for approval, and he spent hours mulling over the trial evidence and verdicts. Almost always he set aside corporal punishment, and he rarely refused recommendations for mercy. Against that, he was stern towards those soldiers who had deserted to the rebels. Despite frequent complaints from loyalists, Cornwallis was not unduly lenient towards rebels. His belief that the 'state prisoners'—those United Irish leaders who had been arrested before the rebellion—could best be disposed of by a full statement of guilt, followed by exile, was probably warranted; and his offer of protection from prosecution to those who surrendered their arms, provided they had not been leaders or had not committed wilful murder, was decisive in bringing hostilities to an end. As for the rest, Cornwallis examined closely some four hundred cases in the months after Vinegar Hill, confirming the death sentence on 81 out of the 131 rebels capitally convicted. In a number of other cases he reduced the period of transportation or imprisonment.

But to those loyalists bent on extirpation, Cornwallis's actions seemed like a sell-out, and criticism of his 'leniency' mounted. In vain he protested:

> I put a stop to the burning of houses and the murder of the inhabitants by the Yeomanry or any other persons who delight in that amusement, to the flogging for the purpose of extorting confessions and to the free-quarters which comprehended universal rape and robbery throughout the whole country. If this be a crime, I freely acknowledge my guilt.

In all, about 1,500 rebels were tried and sentenced for their role in the rebellion in the eighteen months after July 1798. The fate of at least as many more was not recorded. These figures indicate that Cornwallis had pursued a policy of measured severity on his arrival in Ireland, not, as claimed, reckless leniency

The French in Killala, 22 August to 23 September 1798

Throughout the brief, intense weeks of rebellion, the United Irishmen had eagerly, and vainly, awaited French assistance. Dublin Castle too had long felt that disturbances in Ireland 'would probably tempt even a small force from France.' But as the summer passed and the rebellion was crushed, even the Castle's fears receded.

Then, on 22 August, a French force of some 1,100 men under the command of General Jean Humbert waded ashore at Kilcummin Strand, near Killala, County Mayo.

For a brief period it seemed as if the rebellion, by now all but extinguished except in County Wicklow and a few other places, could flare up again.

Humbert's successful landing therefore came as a shock. The general himself was, like Tone's late ally Lazare Hoche, a veteran of the French civil war of the seventeen-nineties, in which the revolutionary government had brutally crushed the revolt in the Vendée. Humbert was not the charismatic, political high-flyer of the style that had made Hoche a rival to Bonaparte himself; yet he had hoped, it appeared, to excite republican ardour in Ireland and, on landing, to persuade the people that France's cause and Ireland's were the same. He also hoped to be reinforced soon, and heavily, by following expeditions from France. On both counts he was to be disappointed. The French forces were delayed at port, and the Irish, it soon appeared, were militarily ineffectual as allies and—in County Mayo at least—half-hearted in their declarations of support for government French style.

Dublin Caſtle, 29th Auguſt, 1798.

ADVICES were received laſt Night from Lieutenant General *Lake*, by which it appears, that early on the Morning of the 27th the *French* attacked him in his Poſſion near *Caſtlebar*, before his Force was aſſembled, and compelled him, after a ſhort Action, to retire to *Holymount*. The Lieutenant General regrets that ſix Field Pieces fell into the Enemy's Hands; but ſtates that the Loſs of the King's Troops, in Men, has not been conſiderable.

A reprint of Lake's embarrassed despatch from Castlebar

The Battle of Castlebar: a later stylisation

If the mere fact of a French landing was a shock to Dublin Castle, a greater one lay in store. The French brushed aside local loyalist resistance at Killala, then quickly secured

Ballina. Picking up local allies, they advanced on Castlebar, routing their march west through the mountains instead of by the Foxford road, as anticipated by General Lake. Very rashly, Lake offered battle and opened fire with his artillery. His was a mixed force of mostly Irish Militia, with English and Scottish Fencibles and some regulars in support. Those rebels who had joined the French promptly ran, but it was not enough to assist Lake. French veterans of Italy and the Vendée were not easily intimidated. Forming themselves into two columns, they bayonet-charged the government force. This time Lake's army broke in panic and fled the field.

General Jean Humbert

Lake had been most unwise to risk a pitched battle with French veterans. It is true that his force outnumbered the French by over two to one (1,700 to 800), but his men were mostly 'half soldiers'— Irish Militiamen—who were probably half-trained as well. Better troops than they had panicked when charged by French infantrymen. As an observer of the French infantry tactics of the seventeen-nineties explained to a Dublin Castle official, 'I have seen so much of the enemy you have to deal with and know so well all the tricks he has in store to terrify those who are not acquainted with them that I shall not wonder if some of your best regiments should be a little astonished at this new kind of warfare.'

A number of Irish Militia who fled the field subsequently joined the French. Lake reported a figure of some 278 men missing after the battle, of whom 158 were from the Longford Militia, 44 from the Kilkenny Militia, and 33 from the Galway Volunteers. A small proportion of these—probably no more than sixty—appear to have gone over to the French. Some of them claimed later that they had joined Humbert under duress, and certainly some deserted from the French soon after. The remainder, however—the great

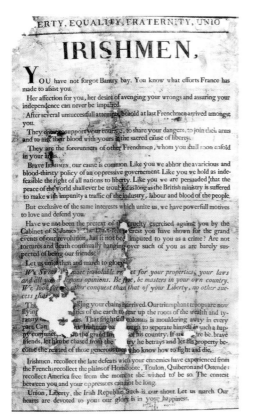

The French proclamation designed to rouse their Irish allies to action

majority—seem simply to have fled in terror and to have taken advantage of the confusion to desert. Almost certainly, many more joined local bands of robbers—abounding at that time—than marched with Humbert.

The results of the battle offered the Castle some further cause for consolation. According to every prediction, the 'races of Castlebar'—for so the battle was maliciously christened—ought to have ignited the whole of Ireland into insurrection. But this did not happen. Isolated rebel forays in Counties Longford and Westmeath petered out, and from Belfast came word that the town and surrounding area remained calm. In the end, the signal victory had turned out to be rather an empty triumph.

In the days following the defeat of Lake at Castlebar, a large force of perhaps twenty thousand men converged on Humbert's army. General Nugent moved his men to Enniskillen, County Fermanagh, to block any move into Ulster; and Adjutant-General Hewett oversaw the assembling of an impressive army from the south and south-east at Portumna, County Galway. A large 'hospital squad' consisting of seven covered wagons with 'hospital bedding, medecines, instruments etc., etc.' left Dublin under escort for Athlone.

In the west, Colonel Craufurd dogged Humbert's footsteps, forcing him south at Collooney, County Sligo, and allowing him no rest. Off the western coast British frigates patrolled constantly in order to see off any French attempt at reinforcing the expeditionary force. Finally,

Bishop Joseph Stock of Killala. Held under house arrest for almost a month, his even-handed account of Humbert's invasion damaged his career prospects.

Cornwallis made his way slowly to Tuam, County Galway, to take command. He justified his 'excess of caution' by pointing out that Castlebar had delivered a salutary lesson and that the rebels and their French allies had to be denied a second victory. Starved of reinforcements and well aware that Cornwallis's force was closing in, Humbert moved north, then east, then ran out of steam. With his Irish allies becoming impossible to control, his own soldiers growing daily more mutinous, with no hope of reinforcements and with little expectation of any significant insurrection in support, surrender was the only option available to him.

Humbert surrenders to Lake at Ballinamuck

On 8 September the French came face to face with the Crown forces at Ballinamuck, County Leitrim. After a short exchange of fire to vindicate national honour, the French force laid down its arms. Honourable terms had been offered to Humbert and his men—indeed the French officers were feted on their arrival in Dublin; but no such terms were offered to their Irish allies. The rebels were scattered 'with much slaughter,' pursued across bogs, and hacked down until the pursuers gave up in simple exhaustion at the task. Others were rounded up and hanged from trees at a local rath known as the Black Fort. Bodies lay bloating in the sun for days in the bogs and hillsides, though the visiting novelist Maria Edgeworth noted in her diaries only the handsome uniforms and appearance of the government troops. It was the last major battle to be fought on Irish soil. The town of Killala itself, first to go over to the French, was stormed two weeks later; rebel losses were put at several hundred dead. As the rebels bled, the French were led in something like ceremony to Dublin and sent away by sea from Ringsend, cheering and singing revolutionary songs.

Some two weeks after the fall of Killala, Theobald Wolfe Tone was captured in Lough Swilly on the north-west coast on his way to join Humbert. Brought to Dublin in chains, he was swiftly court-martialled and sentenced to death. Tone fought for a military execution but was denied it. In a last irony he was granted a brief stay pending further legal argument on his behalf. But it was too late: he had already opted to cheat the hangman by cutting his throat. After days of agony that mirrored those of Edward Fitzgerald six months earlier, Tone died on 19 November.

Even in loyalist Dublin among many who had known him, full of energy, ideas and charm, there was genuine sorrow. Tone's had been the voice that had decisively argued for common cause between Catholic, Protestant and Presbyterian in the heady wake of the French Revolution less than a decade before. At McArt's Fort in 1795 he, McCracken and the others had responded to suppression by vowing rebellion. At Bantry in 1796 the French invasion he had prompted almost shook the British empire to its roots. But when his rebellion finally came, the republican ideal had drowned in blood. With Tone's death, the rebellion was finally over.

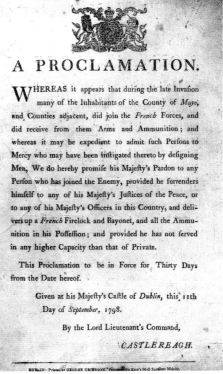

Castlereagh's proclamation promising pardon in return for surrender of weapons in Co. Mayo

Why the rebellion failed

The fall of the Republic of Connacht closed the final chapter in the rebellion of 1798. The rebels had failed because they lacked co-ordination and because, with one or two exceptions, their leaders had had no time to instil even a modicum of military discipline and training into the numbers that flocked to them. In addition, the arrests during the 'pre-rebellion' had been very disruptive, for the rebels thereafter had generally lacked both a leadership structure and a coherent strategy. The result was that it was often difficult or impossible, so the Wexford leader Miles Byrne claimed, to know who had given which order and for what reason. This indecision caused confusion and a loss of morale.

The failure to take Dublin at the outset had been crucial, depriving the rebellion of a focus and preventing the formation of some sort of representative assembly in the capital.

Theobald Wolfe Tone

Castlereagh, the Chief Secretary of Ireland

King George III

143

From that point on, the staggered outbreak of rebellion played into the government's hands: 'We may be thankful', wrote one loyalist, 'that the insurgents have acted so little in unison and have presented us with the means of beating them separately.'

First, the counties around Dublin had risen and been quashed; then, a few days later, County Wexford had erupted and been sealed off; then, Counties Antrim and Down had been tamed. Finally, months later, Counties Mayo and Sligo and areas in Counties Longford and Westmeath had responded to the French invasion force; but by that date it was too late. The failure of the French to intervene decisively had contributed to the rebel defeat. A substantial French force would have offered discipline, leadership, weaponry, recognition, and, perhaps, an overall strategy; the absence of the French had deprived the rebels of all of these.

Finally, and significantly, the rebellion had failed because Catholic Ireland, by and large, had sided with the government. The hierarchy in particular had offered strong support to the government: no word of criticism was voiced of the policy of 'the bayonet, the gibbet and the lash'; the rebels had been immediately excommunicated; and those priests who sided with the rebels—a derisory 70 out of 1,800 in the country—were denounced as troublemakers, drunks, and philanderers. In the inelegant phrase of Bishop Caulfield of Ferns, such priests were 'the very faeces of the church.' The hierarchy had opted to do as they had done for twenty years or more: to be politically moderate in the hope of gaining government confidence and continued Catholic relief. In the end, the bedrock of Catholic loyalty, or quiescence, had helped Dublin Castle ride out the storm.

The government derived some consolation from the fact that the rebellion had been crushed by Irish troops before substantial English reinforcements had arrived. But there was little else to rejoice about. Perhaps 25,000 rebels (including a very high proportion of non-combatants) and some 1,600 soldiers had been slain. Large areas of the country had been laid waste. Such destruction was, wrote one traveller, 'the joint labours of rebellion and of loyalty, soldiers and insurgents making a common cause of devastation.'

A war of religion?

The rebellion was only a few hours old when stories began to emerge of massacre, cruelty, and religious fury. These set the tone for what was soon regarded as a 'Popish plot', a religious war or even a re-enactment of the Catholic uprising of 1641. The ideals of the United Irishmen—even the very name of the organisation—seemed to be swept aside in the confessional fury that erupted in south Leinster. The casual murder of Protestants at Dunboyne and Rathangan in the early days of the rebellion had been followed by the burnings at Scullabogue and the pikings on Wexford bridge in the last hours of the Wexford Republic.

Despite such atrocities, informed contemporaries were wary of seeing nothing but sectarianism in the rising. For every loyalist who saw nothing but a religious 'phrensy' there was another who observed discrepancies and discordances in this picture. Castlereagh claimed that the rebellion was in fact a 'Jacobinical' or French-inspired rising, 'pursuing its object with Popish instruments.' John Colclough of Wexford, whose uncle and fellow-Protestant Cornelius Grogan was hanged for his role in the rebellion, pointed out that 'one can hardly think that it was the original intention of the United men to murder all the Protestants, for many of the heads of them were of that persuasion.' Again, the Castle informer Leonard McNally reported that 'nothing like religious persecution has taken place' in County Wexford.

Crown troops re-entering Wexford at the end of the rebellion

That Protestants were murdered because they were Protestants cannot be denied; nor should the many other instances of naked sectarianism be brushed aside. Such actions were entirely condemned by the rebel leaders. Eighteenth-century Ireland was a profoundly sectarian state, wedded to the principle of Protestant Ascendancy; and developments in the seventeen-nineties had heightened sectarian consciousness everywhere. It was all too easy for evil individuals to exact a personal revenge during the communal disorder attendant on rebellion. But massacre was not rebel policy. The burnings at Scullabogue and the pikings at Wexford Bridge can be attributed to the rebels' collapse of discipline in defeat rather than to a settled plan.

Ironically, the rebellion in the north bore many of the hallmarks of a religious war, for the rebels were largely Presbyterian, while their opponents were adherents of the established church (or Catholic soldiers). In the aftermath of the rebellion, however, this religious division was played down and every effort made to separate the rising in Counties Antrim and Down from the tumult in the south-east. Those Presbyterian United Irishmen who had fought at Ballynahinch and elsewhere consoled themselves in later years with the thought that they had largely acted alone. The promised contingents of Defenders had seldom materialised.

In any case, prudence determined that a veil be cast over the exploits of those Dissenters (Presbyterians) who had espoused the republican cause. Moreover, the Orange Order beckoned. It was reported that by late 1798 large numbers of former rebels were crowding into the order with a view to 'screening themselves.' By the middle of 1799 observers were commenting on the 'astonishing change in the public mind' in Ulster: 'The word "Protestant" which was becoming obsolete in the north has regained its influence and all of that description seem to be drawing closer together.'

This accommodation between members of the Church of Ireland and the Presbyterian Church proceeded very quickly indeed. When Sir Richard Musgrave published his massive history of the rebellion in 1801, so far had amnesia about the rebellion in Ulster developed that he was able to devote a mere twelve pages to events in Counties Antrim and Down, compared with over six hundred pages spent describing the religious mayhem in Leinster. The monochrome interpretation of the rebellion as an onslaught by Catholics on Protestants was thus established. Awkward details about Presbyterian participation and Protestant leadership were not to be allowed to intrude.

Epilogue

The rebellion may have been crushed, but disturbances continued in the years after 1798, notably in County Wicklow, where Michael Dwyer and his band remained 'masters of the mountains,' defying all efforts to capture them or make them surrender. And, despite the failure of 1798, there remained in place (more accurately, in prison, at Fort George in Scotland) a United Irish leadership, which sought to draw appropriate lessons from the experiences of 1798.

Robert Emmet, a brother of one of the leaders of the rebellion, was the leader of those revolutionaries who urged that an insurrection centring on Dublin could have a chance of success. Great secrecy was enjoined on the few who were privy to Emmet's plans: stores of explosives, including rockets, were acquired, and emissaries, among them Thomas Russell, were sent off to make preparations in their own areas.

Michael Dwyer

In the end, ill-luck as much as anything contrived to foil Emmet. An explosion in one of his munition dumps in Dublin in July 1803 forced Emmet and his men to rise up prematurely, and they were easily crushed; but Dublin Castle was shocked at its intelligence failure. Shortly after Emmet's execution, Michael Dwyer, who had been heavily involved in his schemes, surrendered and was subsequently transported to Australia. The 1798 rebellion, it may be said, had had its encore but was now finally over.

4

AFTERMATH

The rebellion was over. Not alone was the physical landscape of Ireland scarred and stained by warfare but the political landscape also had changed. The product and manifestation of that change came in January 1801 in the form of the Act of Union with Great Britain, ending the life of the Irish Parliament, making Ireland formally subordinate to Westminster, and turning Dublin—with drastic social and economic results—into a provincial backwater rather than a proud and bustling capital.

It is the great irony of the seventeen-nineties that the decade that began with hopes of a 'brotherhood of affection' and independence for Ireland ended in bloodshed and the Act of Union. Indeed it was the rebellion that provided the opportunity for the passing of legislation that ended the life of the Irish Parliament.

In the aftermath of the rebellion, understandably, there was much talk of providence and good fortune, lessons, and examples. Lord Shannon hoped that the 'examples made … will give the gentry [i.e. rebels] a surfeit of rebellion and quiet us for 100 years to come.' Others were not so confident of lessons having been learnt. 'The people of Ireland are, and *will long continue* to be ripe for general insurrection,' Colonel Craufurd wrote, adding: 'It is not in the nature of things that men's minds should become less influenced in consequence of the chastisement inflicted on them by the successful part in a civil war.' The former Viceroy, Westmorland, also had his doubts: rebellion has been put down 'for the present in Ireland,' he told the Archbishop of Cashel, 'but unless we can root out the spirit, I fear you will always be suspect upon a favourable opportunity to these explosions.'

Even Cornwallis concluded reluctantly that Britain, for strategic purposes, should consider 'the majority of the Irish people as enemies and employ a large proportion of the force which ought to act against a foreign invader to keep our own countrymen in subjection.'

The 1798 rebellion, and its aftermath, shattered existing relationships within Ireland, awakening atavistic fears and evoking memories of 1641. The very fact that a rebellion had occurred at all had called into question the future of the Irish political structure. Camden's successor, Cornwallis, had been appointed both commander-in-chief and Lord Lieutenant. It was a notable departure from precedent and revealed clearly the close connection between military and political affairs. There was a certain logic, therefore, to formalising Britain's political grip on Ireland to a degree matching the military situation.

And it was a logic that Westminster had long considered. No sooner had the Prime Minister, William Pitt, received news of the outbreak of the revolt than he enquired: 'Cannot crushing the rebellion be followed by an act appointing commissioners to treat for a union?' There was little novel in Pitt's suggestion: such measures had been contemplated during the eighteenth century. As early as 1707, when the union of England and Scotland became a reality, the Irish House of Commons expressed a hope that this would establish a precedent for a more comprehensive union.

The events of the eighteenth century clearly illustrated the difficulty and insecurity of the Anglo-Irish relationship. These tensions, and the trials of managing the Irish Parliament, raised questions of how best Ireland could be ruled. Legislative union was one solution, but within Ireland there had traditionally been little enthusiasm for such measures. In 1759 rumours of a union had prompted riots in Dublin, and almost twenty years later Arthur Young recorded that 'nothing was so unpopular in Ireland as such an idea.'

From Britain's viewpoint, however, union remained an option—one that became particularly attractive in the last quarter of the century as the tumult in the American colonies and the Volunteer phenomenon made the task of government more exhausting. It was, however, the Irish Patriot 'revolution' of 1782—prompted by the demands and

John Fitzgibbon, Earl of Clare, one of the most influential and intelligent of the Dublin Castle administration, was Lord Chancellor of Ireland.

demonstrations of the Volunteers—that really made a union imperative, since many shared the fears of the Viceroy, Temple, that the concessions of that year were 'but the beginning of a scene which will close for ever the account between the two kingdoms.'

This assessment was obviously alarmist, but the reforming, Volunteering spirit that had won the concessions of 1782 made notions of a union repugnant in Ireland—so much so, indeed, that the great nineteenth-century historian William Lecky believed that 'for about ten years after the declaration of independence ... not a single Irish politician or writer of real eminence was in favour of such a measure.'

By the early seventeen-nineties, however, circumstances were more favourable to the prospect of a union. It was not that popular opinion had changed; nor had there been a significant increase in unionist support within the Parliament: it was rather that the concessions made to Catholics had raised fears among ultra-loyalists for the future of their cherished Ascendancy. Of this group the Chancellor, John Fitzgibbon, Earl of Clare, was the most vociferous in his opposition to the Relief Bill of 1793. In his speech in the House of Lords, Fitzgibbon rounded on the Patriots and the 'fatal infatuation' of 1782, which had facilitated the emergence of the Catholic question. There was more at stake, he argued, than votes for Catholics:

> If the principle is once yielded ... it goes directly to the subversion of all civilised government ... If Papists have a right to vote for representatives in a Protestant

Parliament, they have a right to sit in Parliament—they have a right to fill every office of the State—they have a right to pay tithes exclusively to their own clergy—they have a right to restore the ancient pomp and splendour of their religion—they have a right to be governed exclusively by the laws of their own Church—they have a right to seat their bishops in this House—they have a right to seat a Popish prince on the throne—they have a right to subvert the established government and to make this a Popish country, which I have little doubt is their ultimate object.

The very existence of the Ascendancy was in jeopardy. Moreover, the bill endangered the British connection, a nightmare scenario, made worse by the radical temper of Ulster Presbyterians, which prompted Fitzgibbon to moot the possibility of a 'Union with the Parliament of England, as the last resource for the preservation of Ireland.' Behind the fanaticism of his language the logic of Fitzgibbon's argument was clear. Indeed, he

Pitt addressing the House of Commons in London

rightly observed that further concessions to Catholics—ultimately, seats in Parliament—would make the passing of a necessary union practically impossible.

These two anti-Union cartoons showing College Green before and after the Union sum up the arguments of those opposed to the measure.

These sentiments were shared by the Castle administration. In 1797 Lord Camden rejected any further political concessions, on the grounds that 'this country must either be governed according to its present system or that a change more extensive must be adopted.'

1798 moved the question of union into the realm of practical politics. Indeed the rebellion made the union possible, a reality that led to the charge from the United Irishman William MacNeven that Pitt and Castlereagh provoked an insurrection, precisely 'to supply the necessary pretext for effecting their nefarious design.' Such claims are unrealistic. Britain was at war with France and at times in extremis; in such circumstances no government would actively provoke a rebellion. But what is certain is that Pitt recognised in the rebellion an opportunity to promote the union and thus 'provide for the internal peace of the country and secure the connection with Great Britain.'

The rebellion brought home to Ireland's ruling elite the precarious nature of their position. Despite the brave posturing during the eighteenth century, Protestant Ireland was as vulnerable as it had been during the Williamite Wars, and once more its salvation had been delivered by Crown forces, including, as the rebellion went on, heavy reinforcements from England. The British establishment sought to exploit this weakness, and every effort was made to advance the union before peace could induce opposition; even the King approved of 'using the present moment of terror for frightening the supporters of the Castle into a union.'

The task of managing the projected union fell to Cornwallis, ably assisted by Castlereagh. Both were well aware of the likely opposition to the scheme. Edward Cooke, the Under-Secretary at Dublin Castle, advocated the employment of every resource at the government's disposal:

> If you are serious as to union, it must be written up, spoken up, intrigued up, drunk up, sung up, and bribed up; and we must have activity, splendour, popularity, etc. in the administration, exclusive of talent, resource, enterprise, courage and firmness and a few more political qualities.

Opposition to the proposed union created unlikely alliances. It was to be expected that the Patriots, Grattan and the Whigs, would have opposed the elimination of their parliament, imperfect as it was; but the image of ultra-conservatives by their side, including the Speaker, John Foster, was amusing. The conservatives' opposition was based not on constitutional issues, nor lack of attachment to 'the connection', but on their reluctance to surrender their cherished Ascendancy, the unchallenged monopoly of power that a union would end.

John Thomas Troy, the influential Catholic Archbishop of Dublin

The unionist cause too produced unusual combinations—none more ironic than the presence of John Fitzgibbon and the Catholic bishops in the pro-union camp. As the rebellion ended, the Catholic bishops were in fact grateful for its failure. Throughout the seventeen-nineties they had feared that radicalism would damage the process of gradual Catholic relief that they felt their moderation had won. More than that, they feared the militant anti-Catholicism of the French Revolution, which the Irish radicals so admired.

The position of the bishops on the union was complex. While Fitzgibbon favoured a

'Protestant union', politicians in the Castle sought a union on the broadest basis. The Viceroy, dubbed 'Cropwallis' by the ultra-conservatives for being too lenient (in their eyes) towards the Croppies, advocated a 'union with the Irish nation instead of making it with a party in Ireland.' But proposals to include Catholic emancipation in the union package threatened to endanger the entire project; apart from opposition in Ireland, the king himself opposed any 'further indulgences' to Catholics.

Accordingly, an Emancipation Bill would not accompany the union; but the promise of imminent relief was an important inducement to Catholics to support the measure. The Catholic community was well disposed to union; so too were the hierarchy. Archbishop Troy urged total emancipation, informing Castlereagh that 'no arrangement to tranquillise' Ireland would succeed as long as Catholics remained 'excluded from the benefits of the constitution.' Thomas Hussey, Bishop of Waterford and Lismore, declared his preference for 'a union with the Beys and Mamelukes of Egypt to that of being under the Mamelukes of Ireland' (the Ascendancy). Bishop Young of Limerick was the sole dissident in his opposition to the 'annihilation' of Irish independence.

Gillray's brilliant satire on the corruption surrounding the passage of the Union is entitled The Union Club.

When the proposed union was first debated in the Irish House of Commons, on 22 January 1799, the government found itself with a majority of one; two days later it was defeated by five votes. Cornwallis and Castlereagh had not expected this reverse, which brought rejoicing to the streets of Dublin. Foster's carriage was drawn by a crowd through the streets in triumph, buildings were illuminated, and windows without candles were broken, among them those of Fitzgibbon, who was pelted with stones.

Thomas Hussey, the Catholic Bishop of Waterford and Lismore

There was, of course, recrimination on both sides, but Edward Cooke blamed the defeat on Cornwallis's complacency. The Viceroy, he complained, was 'worse than a nobody ... His silly conduct, his total incapacity, selfishness, and mulishness has alone lost the question.' The government, however, would not be deterred from their chosen course. Additional pressure was brought to bear to secure the passing of the union, as tried and tested measures of parliamentary management, argument, negotiation with borough owners, pensions, places and peerages were all applied. As Castlereagh observed,

> those who thrive by the game of Parliament are in general in their hearts against it, and unless connected with their own aggrandizement in some shape will either oppose it or give it but a languid support which encourages opposition in others.

Such measures were effective. When the session of 1800 began Castlereagh was confident of the outcome, and on 1 August the Union of Great Britain and Ireland Act (1800) received the royal assent. The Irish Parliament was no more. The politicisation and turbulence of the seventeen-nineties had made this union inevitable; the alternative was complete separation.

In the absence of Catholic emancipation, however, the Act of Union embodied a fatal flaw, one that eventually transformed the Catholic question into the Irish question. So it was that in the nineteenth century Catholicism usurped nationalism, while the Presbyterians, the Catholics' allies in the 'uniting business' of the seventeen-nineties, defended the union, which had brought them political reform and economic prosperity.

Wolfe Tone's widow, Matilda, with her sons Theobald and Mathew

After the rebellion: the propaganda

Estimates of the numbers killed in 1798 vary greatly. While Dr R. R. Madden, author of a monumental history of the United Irishmen, put the figure at 70,000, contemporary commentators believed that fatalities amounted to 20,000. Of these, perhaps as few as 3,000 were killed by the rebel army. Many victims lost their lives in the bitter loyalist backlash that followed the suppression of the rebellion. The 'brotherhood of affection' was clearly at an end; such sentiments had given way to bitter sectarianism. Indeed it was the divisive nature of religious animosity that had proved effective in sundering the radical alliance of 'Catholic, Protestant and Dissenter'.

Once the rebellion began, the religious card was played to great effect; by the end of

May the country abounded in tales of widespread sectarian massacre. As June progressed, accounts became more grotesque. Events such as those at Scullabogue and Wexford Bridge rekindled folk memories of similar atrocities on the bridge at Portadown in 1641. Loyalist correspondence was full of such details; of the newspapers, the loyalist *Dublin Journal* was particularly vicious in its attack on Catholics, no doubt because of the influence of its editor, John Giffard, who was determined to avenge the death of his 'hero', his seventeen-year-old son, Lieutenant William Giffard, who was killed in the rebel attack on Kildare and whose killing contributed to the massacre of rebels at Gibbet Rath.

These crudely anti-United Irish cartoons are among the earliest attempts to demonise the rising as a mere act of mob violence. They appeared on 13 June 1798, after the Battle of New Ross but before Vinegar Hill.

Loyalists sought to present the outbreak as a Popish plot, a further manifestation of the spirit that had inspired the massacres of 1641. News of rebel excesses in Wexford was grist to the mill, and John Beresford, a member of the Castle cabinet, admitted that such accounts had a 'horrid use; for now there is a flying off of many Presbyterians who were united and the north considers it a religious war.' The *Dublin Journal* continued its assault, carrying details of rebel priests. These were quickly seized on as further proof of the Popish mania that could not go unchecked.

As the war of words intensified, so too did the loyalist backlash. Shortly after his arrival, Cornwallis informed the Duke of Portland in London of 'the folly which has been too prevalent in this quarter of substituting the word Catholicism for Jacobinism as the foundation of the present rebellion.' Like his ill-fated predecessor Fitzwilliam three years earlier, Cornwallis seemed persuaded that discord and violence in Ireland could not simply be explained away as sectarian. It had deeper, and deeply political, roots.

While the Lord Lieutenant declared his intention of opposing bigotry, he was helpless in his attempt to curb the power of the Orange faction, which began to wreak a heavy revenge on the Catholic community. Chapels proved an obvious target for such reprisals, and the burning of the thatched chapel at Ramsgrange, County Wexford, was the first of almost sixty such attacks in the next two years.

These attacks created fear among Catholics. In June 1798 the informer Francis Higgins reported an incident in Francis Street, Dublin, that reflected the tensions in the city.

A disagreeable event took place at Francis Street chapel today. The common people have got impressed on their minds that the government wishes to suppress those Roman Catholic places of worship, which has much irritated and inflamed their minds. A party of Yeomanry passing the chapel yard, some wicked incendiary called out, 'They have come to kill and set fire to the chapel.' This alarm given to an immense concourse of people within, occasioned in the struggle to get to the street, many accidents and the breaking of several legs, arms etc.

DESTRUCTION OF ROMAN CATHOLIC CHAPELS.   351

" A list of the Roman Catholic Chapels burned in the county of Wexford, by the military and yeomanry, in 1798, 1799, 1800, and 1801". From *Personal Narrative of Transactions in the County of Wexford, etc.,* by Thomas Cloney, page 221.

" Boolavogue, 27th May, 1798, - - -	1
Maylass, - - -	1
Ramsgrange, - - -	1
Drumgoold, 21st ditto, - - -	1
Ballymurrin, ditto, - - -	1
Gorey, 24th August, - - -	1
Anacurragh, 2nd September, - - -	1
Crane, 17th ditto, - - -	1
Rock, 12th October, - - -	1
Ballyduff, 19th ditto, - - -	1
River Chapel, ditto, - - -	1
Monaseed, 25th ditto, - - -	1
Clologue, 26th ditto, - - -	1
Killeveny, 11th November, - - -	1
Ferns, 18th ditto, - - -	1
Oulart, 28th ditto, - - -	1
Castletown, ditto, - - -	1
Ballygarret, 15th January, 1799, - -	1
Ballinamona, 18th ditto, - - -	1
Askamore, 24th February, - - -	1
Murrintown, 24th April, - - -	1
Monamolin, 3rd May, - - -	1
Kilrush, 15th ditto, - - -	1
Marshalstown, 9th June, - - -	1
Monfin, 10th ditto, - - -	1
Crossabeg, 24th ditto, - - -	1
Kilenurin, 29th June, - - -	1
Monagier, 1st July, - - -	1
Kiltayley, 10th October, - - -	1
Glanbryan, 13th March, 1800, - -	1
Kaim, ditto, - - -	1
Ballymakesy, - - -	1
Courtnacuddy, 12th August, 1801, -	1
Davidstown, set fire to, but saved,	
Burned, thirty-three Roman Catholic Chapels. **33**	

One Protestant church (Old Ross) burned in consequence of the murder of an unarmed and inoffensive Catholic by the Ross Yeomen".

This list of Catholic chapels burned in Co. Wexford appeared in R. R. Madden's The United Irishmen: Their Lives and Times, *published in 1846.*

Yet just as the Orange bogey had been used to such effect by the United Irishmen before the rebellion, so too rumours circulated that chapels had been burned by the rebels precisely in order to discredit the Yeomanry and rekindle the rebellion. There were also fears in Castle circles that religious animosity might drive Catholics out of the army and Militia.

Before long this initial reaction gave way to a bitter propaganda war, which obscured the original and true political motivation of the rebellion. Simplistic analysis was presented by both sides in an attempt to advance their argument. In loyalist accounts, tales of wanton sectarian attacks were stitched together to illustrate the existence of a comprehensive Popish plot conducted under the slogans of reform and emancipation. Above all, loyalist propaganda was intended as a rallying call to the banner of Protestant Ascendancy, threatened not only by rebellion but by rumours of an imminent union. Protestant strength lay in Protestant unity; as Thomas Rennell, a fellow of King's College, Cambridge, observed, 'whenever the public has been distressed by internal commotions, the strength of popery in Ireland has been fatally experienced.' Such unreliability, he argued, was the hallmark of Catholicism: 'The history of all ages demonstrates what it has actually been. The tenor of events is uniform. The rebellion and massacre in Ireland in 1641, and that of St. Bartholomew in France [1572], and the present commotion in Ireland, all exhibit the same features.'

Such analysis reached its high point in Sir Richard Musgrave's *Memoirs of the Different Rebellions in Ireland*, a huge history of the insurrection, which sought to place 1798 within the tradition of the rebellion of 1641 and the wars of the sixteen-nineties, which had threatened to destroy Protestant Ireland. Once more, Musgrave stressed Catholic unreliability.

It is not what is erroneously and ridiculously called emancipation that the masses of the Irish Roman Catholics want; it is the extirpation or expulsion of the Protestants, the exclusive occupation of the island for themselves and its separation from England.

This he attempted to drive home to the Presbyterians above all: it was time for them to abandon their flirtation with French principles and to end their dangerous liaison with the Catholics. Towards this goal he consciously played up the sectarian aspects of 1798, depoliticised the rebellion in Counties Antrim and Down (which occupied a mere two per cent of his text), and presented it as quite separate from the revolt in Leinster.

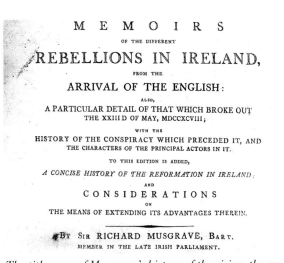

MEMOIRS

OF THE DIFFERENT

REBELLIONS IN IRELAND,

FROM THE

ARRIVAL OF THE ENGLISH:

ALSO,

A PARTICULAR DETAIL OF THAT WHICH BROKE OUT THE XXIIID OF MAY, MDCCXCVIII;

WITH THE

HISTORY OF THE CONSPIRACY WHICH PRECEDED IT, AND THE CHARACTERS OF THE PRINCIPAL ACTORS IN IT.

TO THIS EDITION IS ADDED,

A CONCISE HISTORY OF THE REFORMATION IN IRELAND;

AND

CONSIDERATIONS

ON

THE MEANS OF EXTENDING ITS ADVANTAGES THEREIN.

By SIR RICHARD MUSGRAVE, BART.

MEMBER IN THE LATE IRISH PARLIAMENT.

The title page of Musgrave's history of the rising, the most influential loyalist account of 1798

Musgrave's *Memoirs* were not representative of Protestants in general but rather of an extreme faction within Protestant ranks. As a recent commentator has remarked, it was 'the political bible for a party, not the whole Protestant community.' There were other Protestant accounts, which took a different approach, adopting the line of political conciliation advanced by Cornwallis. This school included James Gordon and Bishop

By the late nineteenth century the revival of Irish nationalism had transformed 1798 in romantic legend.

Joseph Stock, both Anglican clergymen, who consciously sought to defuse sectarianism and notions of a broad conspiracy. Stock might be particularly admired for his broad-minded analysis, given that he had been under virtual house arrest in his palace in Killala during the brief French occupation, forced to listen to an army of newly uniformed peasants firing off their new weapons outside his window.

Arthur O'Connor

There was, however, an economy of truth also on the part of those implicated in the rebellion. The Catholic hierarchy were deeply embarrassed by the presence of priests among the rebel ranks—a fact that Musgrave exploited in his history. Fearing the reimposition of penal legislation, they embarked on a policy of 'damage limitation', in which the active priests were presented as giddy, suspended, or drunkards. It was this insecurity on the part of the Catholic hierarchy that explains their willingness to support the projected union and their guarded approval for the establishment of a royal veto on episcopal appointments.

There were others, too, more directly involved who were equally anxious to dissociate themselves from the political conspiracy. Some sought to avail of the terms of the Banishment Act, under which the authorities offered prisoners banishment in return for full but non-incriminating statements. The result satisfied both parties: the prisoners were spared trials and the inevitable death penalty, while their evidence deprived the rebellion of its political significance. In this way the former United Irish leaders were absolved of responsibility for the rising, which was presented as a response to unrelenting persecution by the Castle administration, an interpretation that advanced Cornwallis's policy of conciliation and the pro-union cause.

The most famous of these statements, the *Memoir* delivered by Thomas Addis Emmet, Arthur O'Connor and W. J. MacNeven in August 1798, laid particular emphasis on the disillusionment created by the recall of Lord Fitzwilliam 'and the re-assumption of coercive measures that followed it.' And, in this propaganda war, the case of County Armagh was particularly significant, because by stressing Orange and Defender violence and government inactivity or terror these former United Irishmen would save themselves from blame. The memoir continued:

> Notwithstanding the greatness of the military establishment in Ireland, and its having been able to suppress the Defenders in various counties, it was not able, or was not employed, to suppress these outrages in that county, which drove 7,000 persons from their native dwellings. The magistrates, who took no steps against the Orangemen, were said to have overleaped the boundaries of law to pursue and punish the Defenders. The Government seemed to take upon themselves those injuries by the Indemnity Act, and even honoured its violators; and by the Insurrection Act, which enabled the same magistrates, if they chose under colour of law, to act anew the same abominations. Nothing, it was contended, could more justly excite the spirit of resistance, and determine men to appeal to arms, than the Insurrection Act.

The rebellion, then, was presented as a spontaneous response to terror, in which the leaders were reluctant rebels. Given even the simple reality that the United Irish had deliberately provoked sectarian fears in some areas to excite support, it was a presentation that was disingenuous even if—in the circumstances—understandable.

Many United Irishmen brought to trial simply denied their membership of the society. In Wexford this argument was plausible, because the county had not featured in United Irish returns seized by the Castle in the spring of 1798. This fact enabled the former rebel Edward Hay in his *History of the Insurrection of the County of Wexford* (1803) to play down political activity in the county and to argue that the rising had been provoked by Ascendancy bigots and Orangemen. 'I am still persuaded', he argued, 'that the insurrection in the county of Wexford was in a great degree occasioned by the conduct of the magistrates, yeomen and military.'

In this depoliticised interpretation of the rebellion, Hay gave a prominence to the Catholic priests who had led their people into the field. By so doing he provides scapegoats for the lay leaders—a fact not lost on Bishop Caulfield of Ferns, who believed

Hay's intention was to 'build a loyal reputation on the ruins of the friars and clergy.'

This selective analysis continued until the eighteen-thirties. Thomas Cloney's *Personal Narrative* (1832) is extremely coy about the author's involvement in the rebellion, while Thomas Crofton Croker's heavily edited *Life* of Joseph Holt (dictated in 1818) completely undermines the contribution of the Wicklow rebel. As much as a fifth of the published text was inserted by Croker, and many of his fictitious additions were intended to depoliticise the original manuscript.

Edward Hay

Ironically, this sanitised account prompted a Carmelite brother, Luke Cullen, to collect recollections from or about participants in the rebellion. These presented an alternative picture of events; it was not that the recollections explicitly mentioned political involvement, but it was taken for granted.

Cullen's manuscripts in turn provided useful source material for R. R. Madden, a Young Irelander who had begun a study of the United Irishmen. This seven-volume history placed the rebels of 1798 back within their French Revolutionary context, the sectarian interpretation of 1798 was rejected, and the rebels were presented as politically conscious freedom-fighters. Madden's account had a profound influence on the Young Irelanders, particularly Thomas Davis, who celebrated Tone as 'one of the greatest men that Ireland ever produced.'

This reconstruction of the United Irish memory received a further boost in 1863 with the publication in Paris of the *Memoirs* of Miles Byrne, the Wexford rebel who had been active in both 1798 and Emmet's rising of 1803. Byrne had subsequently joined the French army, where he rose to the rank of *chef de bataillon* (major); significantly, when he came to retirement he protested at the ministry's failure to include his insurgent activity in Ireland in the calculation of his pension. The *Memoirs* advance the political

This nationalist cartoon entitled The Yeos *recalls the folk memory of Yeomanry terror.
Graphically, it anticipates the propaganda style of the Russian Revolution.*

The apotheosis of the men of '98

interpretation of the rebellion. In correspondence with the historian W. J. Fitzpatrick, Byrne stated his belief that they would 'show the efforts and sacrifices that were made to procure the independence of Ireland.'

Byrne was determined to correct misrepresentations, and he made a sustained effort to rescue the reputation of the few clergymen who had broken ranks by supporting the rebel side.

> How unfeeling and uncharitable and unjust it is of those Roman Catholic historians who have taken upon them to write of the insurrection of Wexford, to condemn, and endeavour to tarnish the reputation of those priests who fought so bravely at the head of the people in their efforts to expel the common enemy.

The timing of this defence was acutely, and intentionally, embarrassing for the Catholic hierarchy. The Fenian movement and the church were by this time seriously at odds. Fenianism, as an oath-bound secret conspiracy, was vehemently opposed by the Catholic leadership. Cardinal Cullen labelled the conspirators 'godless nobodies', and they were subsequently excommunicated.

In the propaganda battle, the example of 1798 was a potent one; and here were priests who could be plucked out of history and into propaganda to personify a clergy—rather than a conspiracy—that could be shown to have given leadership in time of need. The Catholic Church, many churchmen now argued on the basis of 1798, was the body that had 'stood by its people' in the hour of need.

Among the latter was one Franciscan clergyman of County Wexford, who would salvage the reputation of the church and in so doing present 1798 as a rebellion for 'faith and fatherland'—Father Patrick Kavanagh. Kavanagh's *Popular History of the Insurrection of 1798* (1870) ignored the analysis of Cullen, Madden and Byrne and relied largely on local oral tradition. His thesis, which was as much an assault on the Fenians as a history of 1798, was that secret oath-bound conspiracies were doomed to failure. His 'evidence' sought to show that the United Irish organisation was minimal in Wexford in 1798. In this way a case could be made for there having been a leadership vacuum, one into which the clergy had stepped. The truth is more likely to be that, while Dublin Castle remained largely unaware of it, there was indeed a United Irish network in the county. In Kavanagh's analysis, the rebellion was principally a spontaneous popular response to Orange terror and persecution—factors that undoubtedly played a part in bringing much of the population out into the field, but less than the full story. He wrote:

> The people were roused to madness by an oppressive reign of terror by the Orange Society . . . It was in this crisis . . . that . . . a man was found, fearless enough . . . to raise the standard of revolt.

That man, according to Kavanagh's version of events, was Father John Murphy, curate of Kilcormick, near Boolavogue, 'who had opposed the . . . United Irishmen, not from lack of patriotism, but because being a secret society he deemed it unlawful.' The

Father Patrick Kavanagh, the popularising nationalist historian, who did more than anyone to establish the cult of Father John Murphy of Boolavogue

singling out of Father Murphy, who had played a significant part in the Wexford rebellion but never taken overall command, was arguably Father Kavanagh's most enduring intervention. The cult of Father Murphy of Kilcormick owes much to the tensions of the eighteen-sixties and to Kavanagh's work.

Kavanagh's history of the rebellion, which ran to nine editions, salvaged the reputation of the Catholic clergy; but more than this, it created a new, orthodox interpretation of the rebellion, reflected in Patrick McCall's stirring ballad 'Boolavogue' and the sculpture of Oliver Sheppard, which set the tone for the centenary and subsequent commemorations. If the Presbyterians had forgotten their role in the 'Year of Liberty', Catholic Ireland now sought to make it its own.

The struggles within nationalist ranks were reflected in the centenary celebrations. While the Fenians hoped the commemorations would unite all shades of nationalist opinion, within the Home Rule ranks there were bitter jealousies between the Redmond faction and John Dillon's allies—the latter being determined to thwart Redmond's attempt to convert the 1798 commemorations in his native County Wexford into political rallies. Yet despite the rivalry between the various factions within the Home Rule camp, Catholic Ireland presented a united front when over 100,000 people gathered in St Stephen's Green, Dublin, in August 1898 when the plinth was laid for a proposed Wolfe Tone monument. Speakers included the Fenian John O'Leary, W. B. Yeats, John Redmond, John Dillon, and William Rooney of the Gaelic League.

Among the unionist community of Ulster, opposition to such nationalist triumphalism was closely related to their fear of imminent Home Rule. In early June 1898 the Grand Master of the Orange Order condemned a commemoration due to be held in Belfast as

Robert Emmet's rising of 1803 was the last aftershock of 1798 and furnished nationalist Ireland with one of its most potent martyr-figures. The illustration opposite shows Emmet's execution in Thomas Street, Dublin. The one above shows Emmet as mythic figure in the national memory.

a flagitious display of sympathy with an armed insurrection which, above all things, was characterised by a series of most foul and cowardly murders and massacres of innocent men and women whose only offence was their Protestantism.

Such opposition to nationalist display led to a sorry incident in the vale of Ballycreen, County Down. This was the burial place of Betsy Gray, a young County Down woman who went out with the rebels at the Battle of Ballynahinch in 1798 and who was cut down with her brother and her lover. Afterwards she became an Ulster folk heroine and the subject of a popular book. In 1898 a celebration was planned for her grave; but on the eve of the gathering a group of local loyalists smashed her gravestone to pieces. When the Home Rulers of Belfast arrived for the ceremony, the reins of their horses were cut and their carriages were overturned. As one local put it, 'they meant no disrespect to Betsy's memory,' but 'the local Protestants were inflamed because it was being organised by Roman Catholics and Home Rulers. They did not like these people claiming Betsy.'

The divisions evident in 1898 had faded little by 1948, when the new Irish state adopted the by now orthodox view of 1798 to bolster its self-image during the 150th anniversary commemorations. Crowds gathered in Dublin and on Vinegar Hill. Statues of priests and of pikemen in flowing shirts sprang up around Wexford and elsewhere. The songs of 1798, many of them written in the propaganda wave of 1898, joined the canon of Irish balladry. The reality of the late eighteenth century was buried deep.

The bicentenary offers a chance to retrieve something more of the actuality: that it was an age of revolution; that Ireland, a century after the Boyne, was one of many states open to the influence of America and of France; that the political awakening brought about through parliamentary agitation and the Volunteer experience gave rise to the United Irishmen and the idea of a new Irish nation—joined to Britain but distinct and autonomous.

And, ultimately, that the idea failed. Under the pressure of the Anglo-French struggle, London's and Dublin's conservatism reasserted itself with increasing brutality. The United Irishmen chose revolution and war rather than acquiescence. The politics of unity and peace became the practicalities of confrontation and war. And when war finally erupted, in 1798, the deep-rooted divisions in Irish society fed a bloody struggle and then re-emerged even more starkly than before.

There is no simple or comfortable story here. But there is a gripping and important one. The events were tragic, the scale epic. Within them were countless vignettes of great brutality and remarkable courage, often side by side. There were many Protestant rebels, many Catholic loyalists, many Irishmen in red coats fighting Irishmen in green.

These things and many others could not openly be spoken of in Ireland for a generation after they occurred. The simple orthodoxies of 1898 arguably did little service to the truth. The present anniversary offers a chance, if not for a new orthodoxy then for a recognition of the rich and painful complexity that the rebellion and the seventeen-nineties truthfully embodied.

INDEX

Page references to illustrations are in italics.

ACKNOWLEDGMENTS

The Publishers thank the following for the use of illustrations:

The National Library of Ireland; The National Gallery of Ireland; The National Museum of Ireland; RTÉ Library; Belfast Public Libraries; Campbell College, Belfast; Crawford Municipal Art Gallery, Cork; Dr Anne Crookshank and Trinity College Dublin; Mr Jim Doyle, Ardcross; Dublin Public Libraries; Irish Film Archive; Linenhall Library, Belfast; Monaghan County Museum; Public Record Office of Northern Ireland, Belfast; Ulster Museum, Belfast; University College Dublin, Department of Folklore.

bildarchiv preussischer kulturbesitz, Berlin; The Bridgeman Art Gallery, London; e.t. archive, London; Getty Images, London; Leeds City Museum and Galleries; Marie de Paris; Musée de l'Armée, Paris; Musée de la Marine, Paris; National Army Museum, Chelsea; National Galleries of Scotland, Edinburgh; National Maritime Museum, Greenwich; National Portrait Gallery, London; Sir Richard Needham; Public Record Office of London; Réunion des Musées Nationaux, Paris; Royal Collection Enterprises Ltd, Windsor; Victoria and Albert Museum, London.

Pictures and archive research by Gabrielle Brocklesby.